POWER
BORROWING

Other books by WILLIAM PROCTOR

The Ethical Executive with Donald Siebert
The Great Insurance Secret with Sam E. Beller, CLU, ChFC

POWER BORROWING

Sandra Fiebelkorn
with William Proctor

WILLIAM MORROW AND COMPANY, INC.   *NEW YORK*

Library of Congress Cataloging-in-Publication Data

Fiebelkorn, Sandra, with William Proctor.
  Power borrowing.

  1. Loans, Personal.
II. Title.
HG3755.F53 1989 332.7′43   88-31407
ISBN 0-688-06891-X

Printed in the United States of America

First Edition

1 2 3 4 5 6 7 8 9 10

BOOK DESIGN BY MANUELA PAUL

Dedication

To my father, who I know would have been very pleased to see the family name on the cover of this book

Acknowledgments

First of all I want to thank my co-author, Bill Proctor, for enlisting me in this project. He knew that the key motivator in my work is to provide valuable service. This book has given me the opportunity to reach so many more people than I could possibly meet and I hope, help them with a very important aspect of their financial lives. Also I'm grateful to our literary agent, Bill Adler, for his creative skills in initiating the project and putting all the parties together.

One of my goals was to remove some of the mystique associated with credit. Unfortunately, too many financial institutions use terminology that's not only unclear but somewhat intimidating to communicate information about their credit products and policies. These real case histories of consumers like yourself and descriptions of the mechanics of various forms of credit should dispel the mystique. After all, the power and the control in the relationship between lender and borrower should be with you, the aware consumer.

I also wanted to provide you with information that was as practical and current as possible. To do that, I turned to a number of credit experts whose responsibilities involve reviewing and approving credit applications, designing new credit products and services, collecting on past-due bills, and advising consumers who have gone way over their heads in debt. Those experts included Alice Burns of Chase Manhattan Bank, Anne Dunn from NYU's financial-aid office, Luther

Gatling of the Budget and Credit Counseling Service of New York, Niesa Halpern at Sallie Mae, David Kreiss of American Express, Mary Martinson of Master Card International, and Julius Silbiger of Citibank. I also wish to thank Merritt Levine, my accountant, for his insights on the tax ramifications of credit. In addition, I'm very grateful to my editor, Adrian Zackheim, and his assistant, Pamela Altschul, for their editorial help, and to Fafa Demasio for her assistance throughout the preparation of the manuscript.

Finally, I want to acknowledge the customer who came to me to apply for a personal loan when I was managing a branch for Citibank over ten years ago. In the course of our discussion, I asked him, "How much do you need to walk out of the bank with? . . . How much do you think you can afford to pay each month?" He replied, "You sure don't sound like a banker." Judging by the smile of relief on his face, I knew that was a great compliment. We were going to become partners in his financial well-being and that's what it's all about.

—SANDRA FIEBELKORN
November 1988

Contents

CHAPTER 1

A Profile of the Power Borrower

By almost any measure, we are a nation of borrowers. In fact, we're so enamored of debt that it sometimes seems as though we're on the verge of drowning in a flood of red ink—as these recent facts and statistics suggest:

- Servicing household debt now requires more than one third of Americans' after-tax income—up from less than a quarter in 1982.
- More than seven out of ten Americans are in debt to some extent, and many are not meeting their obligations. In 1985, fifteen banks in the United States wrote off more than $1 billion in bad credit card debts.
- The percentage of home loans being foreclosed has nearly doubled in recent years to a post-World-War-II high.
- Revolving credit—which includes credit cards and unsecured personal credit lines offered by banks—increased by 20.3 percent from March 1987 to March 1988.

• At the end of the first quarter of 1988, consumer debt, not including home mortgages, rose to a record 18.8 percent of disposable income.

• Nearly two thirds of all Americans worry about high interest rates on credit cards—yet cardholders charged an average of $2,500 in 1985. This figure was up from $1,900 a year earlier.

Despite the virtual orgy of borrowing that is going on around us, there may be a tendency to say, "Sure, some people have problems with debt. But not me! I know when I'm going too far with credit cards, bank overdraft privileges, and other loans." Even those who admit to problems with debt may go merrily forward with their credit abuse. Too often, there's an assumption that there won't be any consequences for most people who have an unwise approach to debt.

Nevertheless, *anyone* who uses credit or relies on loans is potentially at serious risk. In the years I've spent counseling people about their financial needs and problems, I've learned to take quite seriously the cautionary words about borrowing that have echoed in the writings of a variety of sages through the ages. Listen, for example, to

> *Benjamin Franklin:* "He that goes a borrowing goes a sorrowing" (*Poor Richard's Almanac*, 1757).
>
> *William Shakespeare:* "Neither a borrower, nor a lender be . . ." (*Hamlet*, Act I, Scene 3).
>
> *John Ruskin:* "Borrowers are nearly always ill-spenders, and it is with lent money that all evil is mainly done . . ." (*The Crown of Wild Olive, 1866*).
>
> *King Solomon:* "The borrower is servant to the lender" (Proverbs 22:7).

So who's right—these sages of the past, or we, the debt-burdened ordinary folks of the present? I often hear objections that it may be fine for the philosophers, kings, and literati to pronounce in grand, general terms about the virtues of living frugally and debt-free. But from a practical viewpoint, is it really possible to function without a little abuse of borrowing? Can you have any fun without resorting now and then to too much credit?

Many people I know answer these questions with a resounding no and proceed to live beyond their means. They periodically go overboard with the credit that's available to them by:

- Carrying a revolving balance on their credit cards.

- Borrowing a little more than seems prudent for that three-week vacation.

- Shelling out more than they know they can really afford in order to get a luxury car or a house in the best part of town.

And their attitude is typically, "So what? Is there really anything wrong with living this way? After all, I'm doing it not just for me, but for my family, too!"

In fact, if we're really honest about it, most of us would acknowledge there *is* something wrong with an undisciplined approach to debt. The unbridled use of loans—including relatively infrequent forays into the quicksands of excessive credit—produces an individual that I call the *Weak Borrower*. And Weak Borrowing can seriously hurt individuals and entire families, both financially and emotionally.

I know the danger is very real, because in my work as a banker—and also as an adviser to various individuals—I've seen debt-related disaster strike with devastating power and swiftness. Yet the problems could have been avoided if only those involved had learned how to use credit from a position of strength, rather than weakness. Most of these damaged individuals could actually have come out ahead after going into debt, if only they had been taught how to become *Power Borrowers.*

What is a Power Borrower? This entire book has been designed to give you an in-depth, complete definition of the term. But let me begin by offering an overview of some of the traits that characterize the Power Borrower.

In general, to be considered a Power Borrower, you should first understand the major principles and rules of credit and debt that prevail throughout our society. Then, armed with this knowledge, you should have taken, or at least be capable of taking, steps to:

- Organize a personal or family budget that will maximize your credit advantage.

- Establish significant credibility as a borrower, should the need arise to take out a loan or secure credit.

- Maximize the advantage of bank overdraft accounts and unsecured lines of credit.

- Get the best deals in car financing.

- Maximize credit card privileges without falling into the trap of unmanageable debt.

- Understand the way banks make money from consumers—and learn to take personal advantage of this knowledge.

- Use pertinent provisions in the tax law that can help enhance borrowing power.

- Contact national credit rating services to be sure your credit rating is accurate and puts you in the most favorable light with lenders.

- Make the best use of student loans for yourself or other family members.

- Sidestep the temptation to cosign a loan.

- Consolidate any outstanding loans—to both simplify your repayment schedule and save significant amounts of money in interest payments.

- Use the "float" with credit cards, out-of-town checks and other financial instruments—and thus get what amounts to an interest-free loan.

- Abide by the key financial "commandments" for getting the best mortgage.

Finally, when you have mastered these basics of credit, debt, and personal financial management, you're ready to become more aggressive and use your skills to borrow for investment purposes. Despite restrictions in the latest tax laws, there are still a number of ways to "leverage" your money by borrowing to invest.

In short, the Power Borrower must understand first how to free money for investment. Then, he or she should be able to apply the funds available to their maximum advantage.

In the following chapters of this book, you'll learn how to develop and use each of these skills to enhance your personal financial position. But now, to show you in more practical terms how some of these concepts can work in real life, let me introduce you to one woman whom I'll call Joyce, who began her career as a Weak Borrower. Once she learned to incorporate many of the characteristics of the Power Borrower, her life was completely transformed.

Joyce got a job as an account representative with an advertising firm, and after a few years on the job, when she was in her late twenties, she was making about $50,000 a year. As a single woman with parents and other family members who were financially independent, Joyce had no significant outside obligations to meet, so she had full use of the money she was earning. But still, she always seemed to be scrambling to make ends meet.

"Life is always a financial struggle for me, and I really can't understand what I'm doing wrong," she confided to a friend who did consulting on money management.

After going over her personal financial picture with her consultant friend, Joyce came up with a plan. First, she established a budget. For Joyce, this organizing of her personal income and spending was a completely new and refreshing experience.

"This is the first time I've ever been on a budget," she said, "and I finally feel as though I'm getting control of this part of my life."

Among other things, she decided to wipe out all her debts, which mainly resulted from her free use of checking overdraft privileges and credit card purchases. She used the credit cards to buy new clothes and several meals in relatively expensive restaurants each week. The overdraft privileges typically were used to cover her expenses for elaborate vacations.

When she finally decided to take some action, her total debts from both credit cards and checking overdrafts exceeded $7,000. To make matters worse, she had no source of liquid savings to offset her debts or enable her to respond to any unexpected monetary demands.

The overdraft privileges allowed her to write checks or make cash withdrawals from automated bank teller machines up to a $5,000 maximum, beyond a zero balance in her account; she could in effect take out a loan of up to $5,000 through her checking account. But she found herself relying on this overdraft privilege too often for her own comfort.

"I always felt I was having to scramble to pay off these loans," she said.

By almost any definition, Joyce was a Weak Borrower. Her credit lines and credit cards had mastered her, rather than the other way around. She lived with a nagging sense of guilt that she wasn't taking proper care of her personal affairs. And she constantly feared that some financial "ax" would fall, some major unexpected expense that would require her to come up with money she didn't have.

After she had established a budget, Joyce decided to get rid of some sources of temptation by putting all her credit cards under lock and key in an out-of-the-way drawer in her apartment. She didn't feel she had to go so far as to cut them up, as some credit counselors advise. But she made them inaccessible enough so that she wouldn't be able to make impulse purchases—or for that matter, purchases of any type—without first thinking hard about the costs involved.

Joyce committed herself to writing checks *only* on the amount of money she had in the bank. She elected not to rely at all on the credit line she had through her overdraft arrangement.

There were some "withdrawal" symptoms as she quit relying on debt. For one thing, as she now tried to live within her income—and not within her credit lines—Joyce at first felt that a lot of the fun had gone out of her life.

"I couldn't just walk into a store and buy a new dress or coat," she said. "Now I had to stop and ask myself, 'Can I afford this? Will this expenditure fit into my budget?' "

Gradually, however, Joyce got used to the idea of the pay-as-you-go approach to personal finances. She didn't buy anything she couldn't pay for with cash, or by writing a check on the money she actually had in her bank account. She even forced herself to save a little each month, just to get into the habit.

In short, she moved from an impulse-purchase to a planned-purchase mentality. She no longer just bought a dress on the spur of the moment, wore it once, and then bought another. Instead, she now took more time visualizing and outlining what she needed to complement her existing ward-robe. Before, Joyce realized, she had relied on unbridled spending as a means of making herself feel better when she was "down," and also as a substitute for feeling good about herself. But now, she found she felt much better about herself as she developed an intelligent money-management strategy.

Finally, as perhaps the most important part of her budget, Joyce built in a debt-retirement item, which required her to apply more than $500 a month to getting rid of her outstanding debts. That was a lot of money to devote to her debt payments—for her, it amounted to about one sixth, or nearly 17 percent, of her after-tax income. But she wanted to eliminate those financial obligations as quickly as possible and get off to a new start.

Joyce discouraged herself from falling back into the borrowing trap by reducing her check overdraft protection line from $5,000 to $2,000. This way, she had less capital available if she was ever tempted to overspend again. By reducing her high-interest overdraft credit line, she was in a position to apply for a loan or credit at lower interest rates if the need should arise.

So in a little more than one year's time, Joyce wiped out her entire debt burden. With this achievement, she experienced a tremendous wave of relief that far outweighed any sense of loss she might have felt about having to curb her free-spending habits.

But this was just the first step in Joyce's development into a Power Borrower. Now that she had shored up the weak foundations of her personal finances, she was ready to go on the offensive. At the suggestion of her financial adviser, she continued to take that $500 per month which she had been applying to her debts out of her budget. But now, since she had no debts, she put the money into a savings account. Also, she kept on saving that little extra amount that she had begun to put away while she was paying off her debts. Her total savings came to more than 20 percent of her after-tax income, or more than $7,000 a year!

After about a year, Joyce found herself in a position of growing financial strength. She was debt-free, and had a burgeoning savings account that was fast approaching the $10,000 level. Furthermore, she had just received a raise at work, and she was in a position to save even more money than had been possible before. She decided to sign up for a payroll savings deduction plan that was offered by her employer. This enabled her to put aside 3 percent of her pretax income for savings—*and*, like many plans, the one at her office provided that her employer would match her contribution with another 3 percent!

Joyce was finally in a position to become a Power Borrower. The first thing she decided to do with her savings was to apply the money toward buying a home instead of renting an apartment. She knew that she could get some significant tax breaks through home ownership. Also, she wanted her housing money to go into an equity position in real estate that *she* owned, rather than into what someone else owned.

Soon, Joyce went through the closing on a house in the suburbs near the city where she worked, and she took on a significant amount of debt in the form of a home mortgage. But this time, her foray into debt had been wisely calculated from a position of strength.

Joyce discovered that her reorganized finances still left her with extra money for savings even after she had paid her down payment and begun to make her monthly mortgage payments. So she started looking for other possibilities, such as growth-oriented mutual funds and low-priced real estate that she sometimes bought with friends who were interested in such investments.

This time, she followed a sound rule advocated by many experienced Power Borrowers:

She was only willing to borrow money in order to "leverage" her investment potential. That is, she would only invest in a mortgage on property to be purchased for investment purposes. This way, she could gain an interest in a more attractive building than she could buy just with the amount of money she had in her liquid savings. But still, she always made certain that she could pay back at least 50 percent of the money she owed on any loans or mortgages on property other than her residence out of the cash she had set aside for investment purposes.

In other words, when she had $20,000 in the bank to protect herself, she felt free to go into debt to buy property worth as much as $40,000. With this 50-percent cushion, she felt she would be able to cover any financial reversals that might occur in her investments without having to face a major personal debacle. Also, the 50 percent in savings helped her to meet her debt obligations when they came due each month. In addition, because she took a relatively conservative approach to her investments, Joyce managed to avoid any major declines in the value of any of her investments.

As usually happens with personal investment efforts, not everything she put her money into appreciated in value immediately. A couple of the rental properties she invested in stayed about the same in value over a three-year period, though she did receive income from rents. But other properties in which she had an equity interest increased in value at rates ranging from 6 to 15 percent per year.

Obviously, these increases are not consistent with the get-rich-quick promises made by some flashy investment "experts" these days. But over a three- to four-year period, Joyce enjoyed an overall gain in her equity holdings of from 8 to 9 percent.

Just as important, by borrowing intelligently she was able to protect herself in case for some unexpected reason, the bottom fell out of her investments. In addition, she was consistent and disciplined about the amount of money she put aside for investments each month and also about the amount she borrowed. As a result, she saw a steady increase in her holdings during the first four years that she was a Power Borrower.

Exactly how well did Joyce do in terms of dollars and cents? Her efforts enabled her to move from a position of weakness, as a person who was $7,000 "in the hole," to a person with real estate holdings that had appreciated to more than $50,000 within five years—a definite position of strength!

Of course, Joyce's story, like every other true-to-life account of personal financial development, doesn't really have an ending. In the past, all of her plans have focused on herself as a single person. But now, she plans to get married, and that raises an entirely new set of issues. Many of the principles that she's learned will still be applicable when she and her husband set up their joint household. But there will always be new credit-and-debt challenges to deal with, new personal financial goals to establish and achieve. Also as we'll soon see, the challenges that confronted Joyce may disrupt the personal finances of those who are married or in a variety of other family situations.

The profile of the Power Borrower, then, is a profile that's always changing, always being transformed to enable the individual or the family to deal successfully with personal finances. It's important to recognize the fact that you'll never quite "arrive" in your understanding of this subject. Certainly, you can make significant progress in gaining new knowledge and experience and in strengthening your financial foundations. But flexibility and an ability to grow must always remain essential characteristics of the most powerful users of debt and credit.

CHAPTER 2

How to Go into Debt from a Position of Strength

Before you even consider going into debt, it's important first to establish yourself as a Power Borrower—someone whose personal financial position is characterized by strength rather than weakness. But how do you achieve this position of strength?

One helpful way to begin is by examining the experience of a family that moved from the weakness of excessive debt to personal financial strength—and then began to use debt to enhance their money management and investment opportunities.

One day Sam, who held a city government job, and his wife Lois asked my advice about getting a loan to buy a house. But as we explored their financial situation, it became evident that they needed a great deal of work on their entire personal financial plan before they could even think about trying to get a mortgage.

For one thing, this couple was living in one of the most expensive places in the country, New York City. They were struggling to support their family, including two small children, only on Sam's income of $38,000 a year. Sam and Lois had agreed that while their son and daughter were little, Lois would stay at home to care for them. But this meant that she had been required to give up a job that paid $26,000 annually—an amount that would have solved many of the family's financial problems.

And they did have problems. The couple had sunk deeply into debt: They owed more than $25,000 to various creditors, and the pressure was getting to both of them. Sam had developed high blood pressure and suffered from a number of other physical symptoms of stress, such as a regularly upset stomach. He was more than forty pounds overweight and appeared ten years older than his true age of thirty-eight. As for Lois, her anxieties came out in periodic crying spells. Overall, their marital relationship had deteriorated significantly—and a major cause of their difficulties was their growing burden of debt.

Sam and Lois had never sat down to make up a family budget. Consequently, they had no idea where their money was going. They did sense that they were spending too much on entertainment and on certain other luxury items. But they could never quite put their finger on the main sources of their problems, nor did they know how to take steps to correct their frustrating financial situation.

"How many credit cards do you have?" I asked Sam.

"I don't know exactly. Maybe five or six," he replied. Lois said that she had several too, some for different department stores where she shops.

This family's debts from their credit card purchases came to nearly $6,000. In addition, they had borrowed $11,000 from Sam's mother to buy a car, and they owed another $8,000 to Lois's aunt, who had advanced them cash to pay for a variety of miscellaneous expenses, such as the cost of sending their children to private nursery schools.

Fortunately, there was no immediate pressure to pay back the principal on the loans they had taken out from their relatives, and neither Sam's mother nor Lois's aunt had asked for interest. But far from helping them get out of a financial hole, these loans had just postponed an inevitable day of reckoning. In fact, for a while the loans had lulled the couple into a sense of false security about their finances.

Clearly, this husband and wife are a classic example of the Weak Borrower. So what could we do to get them out of the monetary quagmire into which they had waded?

The first thing they had to do—before they even considered borrowing money to buy a home—was to move into a position of strength in their personal finances. In fact, it appeared to me that no bank would even consider them seriously for a mortgage until they cleaned up their financial act.

"I want you to write down everything you spend this month," I told them. "Put down every penny, and indicate exactly where it goes. I'm perfectly willing to help you, but I can't even begin to give any advice until I know more about your personal cash flow and money management."

When Sam and Lois came in to see me about four weeks later, we all had a much better idea of where their money was going. This family was clearly living well above its income, and much of the expenses they incurred went on their credit cards. Sam took home about $2,200 with overtime during the month that I asked them to monitor their expenses. But the family spent considerably more than Sam made.

Here are a few cases in point for the month that they recorded their expenses:

- They bought more than $200 worth of clothing for various family members.

- The couple spent more than $150 on movies and eating out.

- The entire family spent nearly $200 for fast-food meals and snacks.

- The children received about $70 worth of toys.

- They had to pay nearly $500 on their debts from past credit card purchases. This amounted to nearly one quarter of their take-home pay! Many times, they couldn't pay on time, and more than once, their credit card privileges had been suspended.

With other expenses, including food and rent, they spent nearly $2,700 during the month—or $500 more than their net take-home income. As you might expect, they were unable to save anything in the course of this month. In fact, they had only about $200 in a day-to-day savings account. To top it all off, they were planning a one-week family vacation, which they estimated would cost them about $1,500—which of course, they didn't have.

After evaluating this family's income and expense situation, I advised them to forget buying a house and trying to qualify for a mortgage for the time being. "Any bank loan officer would have to decline your mortgage application. At this point, your financial statements show you can't afford the debt you already have, let alone take on more."

We checked their credit standing with one of the national credit-rating services, and it wasn't good. There were several notations that credit card payments were long overdue. In a couple of cases, credit lines had been closed because he or his wife hadn't paid as agreed.

Obviously, Sam and Lois needed to pay close attention to correcting some of their credit problems and shoring up their financial position. The main thing they needed to do was to get their finances in order by setting up a budget and living within it.

I advised them to structure their budget so that they could gradually pay off their debts, including the loans they had received from their two relatives. Even though Sam's mother and Lois's aunt weren't applying pressure for them to repay the loans, the couple were extremely sensitive to the burden of this debt. As a result, the obligations were putting a strain on their relationships with their well-intentioned loved ones.

Perhaps most important of all, Sam and Lois had to get rid of their credit cards and begin to purchase everything on a cash basis. In their case, because the temptation to use "plastic money" had become so great, I advised them to destroy their credit cards. They went along with this suggestion, though they kept their accounts open so that they could pay off their outstanding debts in installments. Also, they wanted to keep the accounts active in case they decided to ease back gradually into the use of credit cards at some point in the future.

Also, I encouraged them to contact their two biggest commercial creditors to let them know their renewed commitment to paying off their debts in regular monthly installments. Sam and Lois were delighted and surprised at the creditors' reactions. The businesses were understanding and agreed not to put any of the outstanding debts on a collection basis.

With Sam and Lois, the process of moving from a position of weakness to a position of strength was gradual. They had to set strict financial priorities and then cut far back on many of their expenditures that didn't fit into those priorities.

For one thing, they decided it was important to give their children the best education possible. Also, they continued to feel that Lois should stay home with the children, at least until they both had finished first or second grade. In addition to these concerns about the children, they now put a major emphasis on paying off their debts. Finally, they had to make payments for absolute necessities like food and rent. After these expenses had been covered, not much money was left over for anything else.

As a practical matter, their decisions about their finances meant less fast-food meals, movies, clothes, and toys for the kids. Also, they chose to sell their car and rely on public transportation—which fortunately was more available in New York City than it might be in many other American cities.

They used the money from the sale of the car to retire some of their outstanding debts.

All this may seem quite harsh. But as Sam himself said, "What's the alternative? There isn't one!"

So for about four years, Sam and Lois stuck to this Spartan budget, and little by little, their commitment paid off. By the time both children were in elementary school, the couple had managed to whittle away at their debts to the point where they had mostly eliminated their $25,000 in outstanding obligations. Their main strategy had been to pay approximately $480 per month toward retiring their debts and to cut their expenses to the bone so that they wouldn't incur any additional debts.

Most impressive of all, they had achieved this result solely on Sam's salary, which had increased from about $38,000 to $42,000 a year during the four-year period. To be sure, they had felt strapped at times, especially in the first few months of their new financial regimen. But the exhilaration of seeing what they could do with a dose of self-discipline had more than compensated for the pinch they sometimes felt in their family finances.

As a kind of icing on the cake, their new budget had the side benefit of helping Sam to lose weight, get into better physical condition—and lower his blood pressure. By not eating fatty fast foods and by spending more money on vegetables and chicken, rather than expensive quantities of meats and desserts, Sam automatically began to drop those excess pounds.

"At first, I couldn't figure out what was happening to me," he recalled. "I thought I was more worried, or something, and that was what was burning up the calories. But then, I realized that in spending less for food, we were buying and eating healthier, less fattening foods. The reduction in our expenses was actually resulting in the reduction in my weight! That was an exciting bonus for me."

Soon, Sam became so interested in improving on his new

"look" that he embarked on a jogging program—again, something he could pursue at minimal expense. Within the first year on the new budget, he had lost 40 extra pounds. As he got into much better physical condition with his exercise program, his endurance and energy levels increased. Most important of all, he experienced a lowering of his blood pressure to the normal range for his age.

But Sam and Lois weren't destined to have to follow a tough, belt-tightening financial program for the rest of their lives. When both their children had entered elementary school, Lois felt free to return to work, and the salary she was able to command relieved any money pressure the family had been feeling.

At the same time, however, the couple was wary of falling back into their old, destructive, free-spending habits. They had come to understand what personal power they could wield when they took steps to control their debts. So they continued to live carefully and frugally and made plans to buy that home they had always dreamed about.

Before long, they had saved plenty of money for a down payment, and their cash flow was now sufficient to cover the mortgage payments on the kind of house they wanted. They corrected the problems in their credit rating, so when they applied for a mortgage, they were accepted. Furthermore, Sam and Lois now felt completely confident that they could handle this mortgage debt easily because they had learned to borrow from a position of strength, rather than a position of weakness.

To sum up, then, this couple discovered that their life and their borrowing power had been transformed after they had developed several key strengths:

- A sound personal budget

- A strong personal financial strategy, including clear spending goals and an appropriate philosophy of debt

• A solid credit history that earned them a good
credit rating

As a result of becoming strong in these areas, they found
they were in a better position to plan a personal spending
program that involved the use of credit—yet at the same time
accommodated credit purchases to the family budget. Also,
they were better able to formulate intermediate and long-term
financial goals for saving, such as children's education, purchase of a home, and retirement.

Now, let's take a look at each of these "strength positions"
in more detail so that you can understand how you personally
may be able to do your borrowing from a position of
maximum power.

STRENGTH # 1:
A SOUND PERSONAL BUDGET

A major reason that many people get enmeshed in debt
problems is that they have an overly optimistic, fantasy-based
view of what they can do with their available money. But
there's a good antidote to financial fantasy—and that's a sound
personal budget. When you record in black and white what
your income and expenses are, there's little opportunity to
fool yourself about what you can do with your money!

To establish a budget, it's first important to evaluate your
current cash flow, including the relationship between your
take-home income and your actual expenses. So as I suggested
to Sam and Lois, keep track of exactly what you earn and
what you spend for one month.

Carry a small notebook around with you and resolve to
write down every penny you spend, including all the checks
you write.

Next, take a few minutes to evaluate lump-sum payments

you make during the year that may not have come due this month. For example, you may make certain insurance or tax payments only once or twice a year. Or you may take vacations or other recreational trips at times other than in the month that you're monitoring. Also, December may be high on the expense side because of gifts you may purchase for the holidays. Other months may involve an expense "hump" because of birthdays or special occasions.

In general, it's best to figure out the yearly total for those extra, unusual payments. Then, divide each of them by twelve to get the amount of the payment that should be attributed to one month. At the end of the month, group your income and expenses into these categories:

INCOME

• Husband's net earnings (take-home pay, after taxes and other deductions have been taken out)

• Wife's net earnings

• Interest and dividends

• Alimony and child support

• Earnings from other investments

• Income from second job

• Income tax refunds (some families' approach to forced savings!)

• Miscellaneous income

EXPENSES

• Housing, including your total rent or mortgage payments and real estate taxes

• Insurance premium payments (life, property, health, auto, disability)

• Debt payments (for your auto, credit cards, bank

loans, or other debts that are typically paid in installments)

• Household maintenance (e.g., fuel, telephone, utilities, painting, furniture, lawn mowing, snow removal)

• Transportation (commuting expenses and other local travel by bus, train, or private car)

• Food and drink at home

• Entertainment expenses, including such activities as leisure sports, restaurant meals, movies, and hobbies

• Vacations or out-of-town pleasure trips

• Education, including children's schooling and school supplies

• Medical and dental care not covered by insurance

• Clothing purchases and maintenance, including cleaning and laundry

• Gifts and charitable contributions

• Savings, including payroll savings deduction plans

• Miscellaneous

Perhaps you have significant sources of income or expenses that I haven't included in these lists—expenses that are really too large to be lumped under the "Miscellaneous" category. If so, insert a separate line item indicating those expenses, and the amount you've paid.

Then, after you've recorded all your income and expense items, you should figure out the percentage each expense item represents of your total take-home pay. In other words, if your net take-home income for the month is $2,400 and you pay $600 a month in rent and other housing-related costs, your housing percentage would be 25 percent of your total expenses.

Is there a "right" set of percentages for your expenses? Obviously, each person and each family has distinctive needs and obligations. Also, we have different value systems—a fact that helps determine where our money will be spent.

As a result, it's impossible to be absolutely definitive about the percentage that you should be paying for food, housing, or whatever. But still, some sound budgeting guidelines have emerged in the thinking of many financial counselors, who have helped a variety of people formulate a solid, successful personal budget.

For example, here are some suggested percentages of after-tax, take-home pay that I've discovered often work well for those who want to establish themselves as good money managers—and Power Borrowers. I'm assuming an average after-tax take-home pay of $36,000 for a family of four people.

RECOMMENDED PERCENTAGES OF TAKE-HOME PAY FOR FAMILY EXPENSES (FAMILY OF FOUR—ANNUAL AFTER-TAX TAKE-HOME PAY: $36,000)

• Housing, including your total rent or mortgage payments and real estate taxes—28 percent

• Household maintenance (e.g., fuel, utilities, painting, furniture)—7 percent

• Insurance premium payments (life, property, health, auto, disability)—5 percent

• Debt payments (for your auto, credit cards, bank loans, or other debts that are typically paid in installments)—1 to 6 percent

• Transportation (commuting expenses and other local travel by bus, train, or private car)—15 percent

• Food and drink at home—14 percent

- Entertainment expenses, including such activities as leisure sports, restaurant meals, and movies—5 percent

- Vacations or out-of-town pleasure trips—4 percent

- Education, including children's schooling, school supplies, music lessons, and camps—2 percent

- Medical and dental care not covered by insurance—3 percent

- Clothing purchases and maintenance, including cleaning—6 percent

- Gifts and charitable contributions—5 percent

- Savings, including payroll savings deduction plans—5 percent

- Miscellaneous—5 percent

Keep in mind, however, that these percentages only represent generalizations about what allocations of incomes will work for many families. They certainly won't be right for all families. Here are a few common variations I've run into:

- You may decide that your home, its furnishings, and other physical surroundings matter a great deal to you—more than you can buy with only 7 percent of your income. So you may decide to cut back on clothing or vacations and put extra cash into your house.

- You may find that because you have a considerably higher take-home pay than $36,000—say, $50,000—you are able to allocate a much lower percentage than 14 percent to your food bills. So you spend only about 9 percent of your disposable income on your at-home food, and you put extra cash into your vacations.

- If you live in a high-rent or expensive real estate area like Manhattan, Los Angeles, San Francisco, or Chicago, you'll probably have to pay more than 28 percent for your housing.

- If your children are in private school, you may be paying much more than 2 percent of your after-tax earnings for their education.

Clearly, then, not every individual or family is going to fit into the percentages I've suggested. But in general, these figures provide a fairly good starting point to establish your guidelines for a personal budget. Also, anyone who can organize his or her personal affairs along these lines will be in a position of strength to become a Power Borrower.

For example, as we'll see later, if you want to be in a strong position to seek a mortgage for a house, many bankers will want you to be able to handle the mortgage costs and real estate taxes by spending no more than 28 percent of your net income. And these lenders may ask that your other indebtedness amount to no more than 6 percent of your net income. As you can see, I've recommended that your installment debt payments be even lower, at 1 percent of your net income.

In short, if you use these percentages as basic guidelines, even as you tailor these proposed budget categories to your individual needs, you should find that your financial strength—and your ability to borrow effectively—will increase. But a budget is just the first step.

STRENGTH # 2:

A SOUND PHILOSOPHY OF DEBT

The foundation for a sound philosophy of debt begins with learning how to respond to debt-related danger signals in your personal finances. Then, when your money problems have been resolved, the way will be cleared for you to take positive steps to become a Power Borrower.

To achieve these objectives, here are some rules of thumb that can put anyone on the road toward Power Borrowing. Most of these points will be covered in more detail later in this book. But even now, you can begin to use them as a handy checklist of "commandments" to start getting your financial house in order.

Commandment 1: Your ultimate goal should be to spend 1 percent or less of your after-tax income on personal debt payments (not including mortgage payments on your home or payments for investment property). So, if your take-home pay is $50,000, your objective should be to spend no more than $500 annually to repay principal and interest on personal debts like installment purchases for credit cards. *Note:* This percentage only applies to those debts that carry interest—not to credit card purchases or other payments that you make within a grace period and that carry no interest.

Commandment 2: Set an outside limit of 6 percent on your personal debt repayments. A 1 percent personal-debt-payment level is a very difficult, if not impossible, goal to achieve. So, as a kind of fall-back position, I suggest 5 percent as an absolute outside personal-debt-payment limit. In fact, I believe that no one can be a true Power Borrower and spend more than 5 percent of after-tax income on personal debt payments. This means if your take-home pay is $50,000, you should be spending no more than $2,500 annually in paying back principal and interest on your debts. Furthermore, if you're spending more than 15 percent of your after-tax income on personal debt payments, you're heading for big trouble and should seek credit counseling.

Commandment 3: Recognize that it usually takes an average of eighteen months to two years for those in serious debt to pay off their obligations and put their finances in proper balance. Many experts feel that if you can't clear up your debts within three years, you're probably heading toward bankruptcy.

Commandment 4: Do the obvious: Build a solid credit history by paying off your obligations on time. This practice will establish a good credit rating that should be reflected in the records of the major credit-rating services.

Commandment 5: Limit your personal housing payments (including all outlays for rent, mortgage, or real estate taxes) to no more than 28 percent of your after-tax income.

Commandment 6: Be sure you're observing the 28–34 rule: That is, spend no more than 28 percent of your after-tax income on personal housing payments and no more than 6 percent on other personal debt. (As you'll see later, many banks follow this rule in determining how much of a mortgage they're willing to give those who want to buy a house. If you're observing Commandments 2 and 5, you'll be well within this commandment.)

Commandment 7: Despite all the pundits who claim they can show you how to put "nothing " or "next to nothing" down on a home, be prepared to pay 20 percent of the purchase price as a down payment. That way, you'll be in a position to get the best interest rates.

Commandment 8: If you're self-employed, you may have problems proving your income to a bank's satisfaction for a mortgage application. Usually, they require two years of the business financial statements or income tax returns. But if you've been aggressive in claiming deductions to show a loss, don't expect the bank to regard you as a good risk. On the other hand, if you can make a down payment of 25 percent or more of the purchase price, some banks will accept your income as you state it.

Commandment 9: Always be wary of low "come-on" rates offered by many banks for mortgages. In most cases, the fine print will show you'll have to pay more than you bargained for within six months to a year of getting your mortgage.

Commandment 10: If you take out a home equity loan, use the money for conservative investments, not for living expenses. If you spend the loan on your living expenses, such as entertainment, vacations, or food, you may find yourself in danger of losing your home.

Commandment 11: Always shop around before you take out any loan or credit line. Ask plenty of questions and analyze the implications of the various interest rates and payment schedules. Make sure your monthly cash flow can comfortably accommodate the new monthly payments. Basic good consumer judgment applies with banks, as with any other business.

Commandment 12: Shop around before you settle on a credit card. Check grace periods, finance charges, and any other factors that may increase the cost of your "plastic money."

Commandment 13: Try to save at least $5,000 to $10,000 a year for investment purposes. Accumulate this money in a savings or money market account until you find the investment vehicle that you want.

Commandment 14: When you're debt-free and have saved at least $10,000 for investment purposes, begin to leverage your investments with the "50-percent rule."

Simply stated, this rule says that when you're investing,

you should always be sure that at any point, you can pay back, out of the cash you have on hand, at least 50 percent of the money you owe on investment loans. So, if you have $10,000 in the bank to protect yourself, you should be able to go into debt to buy property worth as much as $20,000.

Commandment 15: Always focus on the investment value of your investments, not the tax breaks you hope to receive from them.

Commandment 16: Borrow, if you must, as a student—but shop around at the different agencies and be as conservative as possible in going into debt. Remember: These days, there's no place to hide when the government comes collecting on student loans! (More of this in Chapter 8.)

Commandment 17: It may be best to use the cash advance feature on bank cards, rather than the checking overdraft privileges. One recent spot check showed a 6 to 7 percent lower rate for some cards than for the overdraft privileges.

Commandment 18: Bankruptcy will affect your credit rating, your borrowing power, and your personal finances for up to ten years. So avoid it!

Commandment 19: When you decide to borrow money, check your own bank first. Your own banker is likely to give you the best rates.

Commandment 20: Many times, you can get the best deals on car loans and car purchases if you are willing to take models off the floor, rather than order cars with special accessories.

Commandment 21: Get in the habit of paying within the grace period on your credit cards, rather than paying over time and incurring interest and finance charges. Remember:

Interest payments on most installment debt and credit card purchases are only minimally tax-deductible.

Obviously, there are many other "commandments" that might be listed to promote a wise use of debt and credit. As we move through this book, other guidelines will emerge to help you in your effort to become a Power Borrower. But for now, these twenty-one should be sufficient to give you an idea of what a sound philosophy of debt must involve.

STRENGTH # 3:
A SOLID CREDIT HISTORY

Before you can become a Power Borrower, it's necessary to achieve a good credit rating. And a good credit rating depends heavily on a solid credit history.

Having a good credit rating means you are considered a good risk by various lending institutions, such as banks. If you borrow money from them, they expect that you'll pay it all back—and pay it back on time.

Many times, you can get a line of credit, or be assured that you can borrow a certain amount of money, simply by showing that you have a substantial income or substantial financial assets. But having a large income or large investment holdings doesn't necessarily mean you have a good credit rating. Indeed, I know a number of people with very large incomes, but poor credit ratings and a limited ability to borrow—because they have compiled a questionable or weak credit history.

One two-career couple, Bob and Mary, were grossing about $70,000 a year, but somehow, they never seemed to have enough money. In fact, they sensed they were paying as much on their credit card bills and bank credit lines as they were on the necessities of life, like food and shelter. I say they "sensed" this because they never bothered to sit down and analyze their situation—at least not until a personal financial crisis struck them.

The crisis began in the form of an inability to pay a group of credit card bills that came in with "final notice" plastered all over them. In some cases, there were also notices of impending suspension of credit privileges. The last straw for Bob was the embarrassment of trying to charge a purchase for his daughter in a toy store and having the salesman report that his credit card was no good.

"I couldn't believe it," Bob said in a financial counseling session just after these incidents. "We make more money than most people, yet we can't even buy a cheap little toy for our child!"

In fact, Bob and Mary had a great deal of company with their financial problems. According to one in-house Citibank publication, 21 percent of families with incomes of $25,000 and above spend 5 to 9 percent of their gross income on making installment payments; 8 percent in this income range spend 10 to 19 percent of their gross income on installment debt; and 2 percent spend an incredibly burdensome 20 to 39 percent on such debts.

Bob and Mary were spending nearly 18 percent of their gross—or about $12,600 annually—on their installment debts, which totaled more than $30,000. That had been enough to precipitate their credit crisis and force them to seek outside help.

During the counseling sessions, they checked their credit rating with TRW Inc., a national credit bureau. To their chagrin, they found that their credit standing had been impaired because of a failure to meet their obligations. One credit card company had already canceled its plastic charge privileges and was threatening to sue. Several other companies were apparently on the verge of taking similar action. Until the couple cleared up these debt problems, it would be difficult for them to qualify for other credit lines and loans, including one for a country house they hoped to buy.

On the verge of panic, Bob and Mary readily accepted the advice of their financial counselor to place a top priority on getting themselves out of debt and rebuilding a sound credit history. This meant taking several essential steps with their credit and creditors. They had to:

- Immediately stop buying on credit.

- Begin living completely within their incomes—even though that meant postponing a vacation they had planned and reducing all unnecessary personal purchases, including those extra toys for their young daughter.

- Notify their creditors that they were turning over a new financial leaf.

- Try to work out debt repayment schedules that they could live up to.

These were bitter pills for Bob and Mary to swallow, especially since they had been free spenders for years. With their healthy family income, they had *expected* to be able to spend pretty much as they wanted. It was a rude shock to learn that there were definite limits on how far their money would go. But eventually, over a period of about a year, they were able to achieve a better financial balance.

To be sure, they weren't able to get themselves completely out of debt in one year's time. Obligations amounting to over $30,000 require more time than that to liquidate on a $70,000 annual income. Still, Bob and Mary managed to get back on a regular repayment schedule and make significant inroads in retiring their debts in a year. For them, that was quite an achievement. Now, they are in a position to pay off their outstanding debts over a couple of years and then to begin to borrow as Power Borrowers, rather than Weak Borrowers.

Their credit standing has already improved with a number of businesses, and I expect that within two to three more years, they will establish significant credibility as borrowers. *Note:* Some "bad marks" may remain on the records of credit bureaus for up to seven years. But Bob and Mary acted quickly to correct their problems, before any legal judgments were rendered against them. I expected that their less serious offenses, such as late payments and one instance of cancelled credit card privileges, could be overcome in a couple of years by demonstrating, through a clean credit record, that they had turned over a new leaf.

But of course, it's best never to get into the situation that this couple faced. Try to take steps as early as possible to establish a solid credit history and with it, a good credit rating. But what's the best way to achieve these goals?

To answer this question, let's delve in more detail into what it means to achieve and maintain a strong credit rating.

CHAPTER 3

A Simple Strategy to Achieve a Good Credit Rating

Not all debt is bad or destructive. Indeed, the whole idea of Power Borrowing is based on the premise that some types of debt can be *productive*—if you can arrange things so that you go into debt from a position of strength, rather than a position of weakness.

But still, some debt can be extremely destructive to a person's financial standing, and even to his character. To avoid this kind of debt—and to formulate an effective strategy that will lead to a good credit rating—it's necessary to follow several basic principles, which at first glance, may seem so obvious that they're not really worth mentioning. But believe me, most people don't follow these guidelines, no matter how simple and self-evident they may seem.

Principle 1: Severely restrict your reliance on credit

This first principle is the soul of simplicity: You just limit your reliance on credit cards and loans so that you can always pay back your obligations out of current income.

Probably the best way to make this principle a practical part of your life is to think in very concrete, down-to-earth, dollars-and-cents terms. As I've already emphasized, payments you make for installment debts, not including mortgage payments, should never exceed 5 percent of your after-tax income. Preferably, these debt payments should be limited to about 1 percent of your after-tax income.

In the case of Bob and Mary, whose situation has been described previously, installment debt payments consumed about 18 percent of *before*-tax, gross income. At their tax rate, this amounted to about 25 percent of after-tax income!

As Bob and Mary discovered, it's not so easy for many people to follow this first, seemingly simple guideline. One of the great pitfalls that causes many to stumble and fall into a major credit trap is the sneaky, deceptive character of credit and debt in our society.

Advertising and the mass media make us intensely aware of the use of money by the "rich and famous," and the "in crowd," or the scions of "society." Then somehow, the expectation is communicated that *everyone*, regardless of financial means, can have a taste of this same luxurious life.

Simultaneously, there seems to have been a lack of solid, authoritative guidance these days about the responsible way to organize personal finances and manage family money. In the past, the idea of the stewardship of one's finances was more acceptable: That is, many people made the assumption that they had received their money or money-making talents from God for a broader purpose. So it was up to the individual citizen to be circumspect and responsible in organizing and dispensing his or her personal funds.

Today, in contrast, the prevailing ethic seems to revolve around such materialistic maxims as:

- "Spend now, pay later."
- "Buy what you like, not just what you need."

- "I *deserve* to own what those people have (or do what they're doing)."
- "Why save? You can't take it with you!"

The adage "Eat, drink, and be merry for tomorrow you die," once criticized by moralists (and rooted in the revered warnings of Ecclesiastes, Isaiah, and Luke), has now become a slogan *de rigueur* for free spenders of every social stratum.

Granted, it's difficult to break free of such strong and seductive cultural siren songs. After all, we no longer have to worry about debtors prisons. And personal bankruptcy sometimes seems almost to be a rite of passage that many, including even some of our finest and brightest, must endure. Consider, for instance, the financial fiascoes of the recent secretary of the treasury and aspiring presidential candidate, former Texas governor John Connally. After reaching a seeming peak of material and professional success, he found himself facing the sale of his prized personal assets to satisfy his creditors.

But none of these debt-related problems is inevitable. There *are* ways to escape this deceptively well-paved path to destructive debt. One of the most effective means of deliverance is to begin as soon as possible to develop the good habits associated with achieving a solid credit history that leads to a good credit rating.

Principle 2: Develop healthy borrowing habits

If you want to establish yourself as a Power Borrower—and protect yourself from the temptation to slip into excessive, destructive debt situations—an important initial step is to develop healthy, disciplined personal borrowing habits.

If you're a person who has no experience with credit, you'll have to get some experience by wisely and judiciously showing that you know how to use and repay other people's money. Or if you've already had access to credit but have somehow gotten mired down in debt problems, you'll have to extricate yourself first. Then, you'll have to develop some better habits that show you've repented of your profligate ways and can now be depended upon to borrow only the amounts you can manage. And that means showing you can repay your obligations on time.

To understand how to develop good borrowing habits, assume for the sake of argument that you have little or no borrowing experience. Obviously, most adults in our society with any experience as consumers usually have some sort of credit card, credit line, or involvement with loans. But there are also millions of adults who don't have a credit card or other borrowing experience. There are also many young people who have not yet become involved with credit and debt.

Those who have no experience with credit and debt can begin to establish good personal borrowing habits—and simultaneously to signal to potential lenders that they are responsible money managers—first by setting up a credit account. Then, they have to demonstrate that they know how to use it carefully and responsibly.

For example, you might apply for a credit card with a retail department store or a Visa or MasterCard at your local bank. Then, you should make a few purchases with the card, but *be sure* to pay the bills when they come due!

I make this suggestion to nonborrowers with great caution and even trepidation, however, because I know what a slippery slope credit cards, credit lines, and bank overdraft arrangements can create. Most people begin to use their credit privileges without the foggiest notion of the dangers that lurk therein. They have no personal philosophy of debt, and as a result, they often fall prey to excessive consumption and the tendency to live beyond their means.

On the other hand, those who have never undergone this "baptism of credit" may find that they face roadblocks to taking out a loan when they need it because they've failed to establish a credit history: That is, they've never demonstrated that they know how to borrow money and pay it back.

Without such a track record, it's difficult and sometimes impossible to convince a bank or other lending institution that you're a reliable credit or loan risk.

One husband and wife I know decided to get their young teenage son on the road to establishing a good credit history so that, in the words of the father, "he can qualify for his own American Express card by the time he enters college." (If this seems a premature goal, consider another couple with an even more ambitious plan: They wanted their elementary school son to have his own American Express charge card by the time he was twelve!)

I don't know how the second couple has fared, but the first proceeded to get their boy a store retail card and a service station credit card when he was sixteen. Soon afterward, he got a bank-issued national credit card. This teenager held down several good paying jobs during this period and also made purchases on his card—and was always conscientious about paying his bills on time. Finally, right on schedule, he applied for an American Express card during his first year of college—and his application was accepted.

In the process of developing a healthy credit history, this young man has learned some good lessons about the best way to manage his money. Now, he's well on his way to becoming a Power Borrower.

Any adult who is just beginning to get involved with credit and debt would do well to follow this youngster's pattern in developing a healthy credit history. For that matter, many other adults who have already been involved with credit in the past, but have "blown it" through poor borrowing habits, can also learn some valuable lessons from this example.

It's never too late to change your ways and embark on a course of conduct that will establish you as a good credit risk. Perhaps you've abused their credit privileges to some extent. Or you may have gotten far over your head into debt, and now you have a *bad* credit history, based on *bad* debt habits. Our earlier example involving the couple, Bob and Mary, illustrates this point. But as the case of Bob and Mary also shows, there's a way out of this mess if you'll just begin *right now* to follow good borrowing habits instead of bad ones.

To sum up, then—whether you're a person who is starting out with no credit history, or a person who has developed a poor track record with debt over the years— there are several basic habits you must develop if you want to establish a healthy credit history. These include the following:

- Develop a track record of credit; make sparing use of one or two credit cards, or perhaps a loan service, such as a bank overdraft privilege.

- Pay off any installment debt obligations you incur as quickly as possible—in one, initial payment when you receive the first notice, if you can manage it. That way, you'll achieve two important objectives: (1) You'll avoid unnecessary interest or finance charges, which are now only minimally tax-deductible. (2) Also, you'll reduce the chances that your total indebtedness will increase beyond what you can manage to repay on your current income.

- If you can't pay all or most of your obligations when you get the bill, at least pay the minimum due on your loans or credit cards. And be sure that your payment *arrives* at the lending institution or store by the due date indicated in the statement. Paying consistently within forty days rather than within the twenty or so days that your credit agreement calls for, is the first step toward an unfavorable credit rating.

- If you get behind in your payments or run into other problems with a credit card company or lending institution, don't allow the situation to fester. Get on the phone immediately with the lending institution, explain your difficulty, and enlist the lender's help in correcting the situation.

• If necessary, *negotiate* with your lender to improve your credit standing.

Sometimes, it's not possible to repay all the money owed by the time a lender wants it. Perhaps the borrower—and that may include many credit card users, like Bob and Mary in our earlier illustration—just accumulates too many debts from too many sources. Suddenly, he realizes he can't make all the payments that are due, and he panics. But often, if the strung-out borrower will just call up one or more of the lenders, he'll be able to work out something and reduce the negative impact on his credit rating.

One person sitting in the delinquency unit at American Express overheard just such a negotiation take place. Under the terms of agreement for the issuance of the American Express card, the entire amount owed had to be paid at once. Granted, according to the company's customs, you could wait forty-five days or even longer to pay. But when you paid, you had to remit the whole amount owed.

An American Express cardmember called because he was unable to meet the entire month's payment, and the understanding company representative had some helpful suggestions:

"Do you hold one of the bank cards, which allows you to borrow money and then pay it back over time?" the company representative asked.

The borrower answered that he did, though the amount he could borrow wouldn't cover the total amount of his debt to the company. Still, the company representative suggested that he take out a loan on his bank card and pay off as much as he could of the American Express debt.

"I'll see if we can arrange a payment schedule for you to repay the rest of what you owe over the next few months," the representative said.

Typically, a credit card company will allow up to six months for a delinquent cardholder to pay off his debts. (It's best not to take advantage of such an arrangement unless you have to, however, because your failure to pay on time will most likely be reflected in the records of a credit bureau.) In the American Express cardmember case, the borrower would also have had to pay off the amount he had borrowed as a cash advance on the bank card.

Obviously, this solution was just a stopgap measure and could easily turn into a "robbing Peter to pay Paul" situation unless the borrower quickly got his personal financial act together. Also, the proposed solution clearly favored the company whose representative was making the suggestion. But still, by communicating and negotiating with the lender, the borrower took a step in the direction of resolving his debt problems.

• Finally, to build or *re*build a good credit rating, it's important to check periodically with a major credit bureau that keeps track of your credit standing.

Principle 3: Monitor your credit rating

In general, you can't get a "credit rating" as such from various credit bureaus. In fact, one of the major bureaus, TRW Inc., states explicitly on its reports: "TRW does not provide general credit ratings or make credit granting decisions."

But you can find out what specifics of your credit history are on record and thus identify potential problems with your credit standing before you apply for loans or credit. The major credit-monitoring services include TRW, Chilton, Trans Union, and a few others. To find out how you stand, all you have to do is write them, pay the modest fee they require (usually about ten dollars), and ask them for your credit file.

When I wrote TRW to get my file recently, I found that they had included all of my current major credit accounts. But they had also listed some credit card accounts as "current" that I had actually closed.

In a survey of these credit bureau services, the staff of _Forbes_ magazine (August 24, 1987) also encountered some discrepancies and omissions in various credit bureaus' files. For example, heavy debt obligations like mortgages usually didn't appear in the files. Also, student loan obligations didn't appear.

In addition, one of the journalists found that TRW had no record of his Visa, Diners Club, Bloomingdale's, or Foley's credit accounts. On the other hand, the bureau did list an account with Sanger Harris Department Stores—though he hadn't bought anything there in three years. Information on credit balances and employment was also out-of-date.

A representative of TRW responded that information on mortgages usually doesn't appear in the credit records because people typically pay on their mortgages before they pay on anything else. Also, creditors tend to report to TRW at different times, so some of the figures recorded may be out-of-date.

As for employment information, the credit bureau usually records your employment at the time you apply for credit, but the bureau may not update that information unless you apply for credit again. Finally, certain old accounts—which you may assume have been closed—may still be reflected with the credit bureau because companies like department stores often keep inactive accounts on their records.

In any case, with all their deficiencies, credit bureau records are an important part of your credit history, and you should be aware of what information is contained in them. Here are a few tips to keep in mind for interpreting your credit record—and for keeping it as clean as possible:

- A court judgment against you can be a serious blot on your record—so avoid legal consequences from indebtedness whenever possible. But there are judgments—and there are judgments. For example, a $200 judgment won't usually be regarded as seriously as a $2,000 judgment. Also, a judgment that occurred six years ago won't carry as much weight as one that happened one year ago. A problem that involves a department store credit card probably won't be as significant as a problem with the Internal Revenue Service. Many banks and other institutions looking at your credit file will be willing to listen to your excuses for failing to make a disputed department store purchase—but they won't be so understanding about the IRS.

- Your credit history will usually go back about seven years. Any credit activity or problems before that date will typically be lopped off your records.

    In other words, you have a chance for a "clean credit slate" every seven years. So take advantage of this fact if you currently have negative, harmful entries on your record: Begin to "live right" *now*. Soon, within a few years, you'll find you have a clear record, and your credit standing should improve significantly.

- If a credit problem is reflected on your credit bureau records and it's incorrect or there's something you think you can do about it, clear it up immediately.

The first step is to try to straighten the situation out with the company or organization with which you have the problem. Then, you should get a representative of that company to notify the credit bureau that the problem has been corrected. Finally, follow up to be sure that your credit record has cleared.

• If you take a relatively long time to pay a credit card bill or loan notice, that delay may not be reflected negatively in your credit bureau records.

For example, certain credit cards may allow you sixty days to pay your bills before they start sending you serious collection notices. In general, as long as you pay consistently before the final collection deadline, your credit bureau record will stay clear. Credit card companies in particular look for your *normal* payment behavior. So if you're normally a late—but a consistent payer—you'll probably never have a problem.

But let me caution here that I'm not recommending that you wait until the last minute to pay your bills. Such a practice may work for a time, but eventually, most people slip up: They inadvertently file a bill without paying it. Or they are out of town on a vacation when the final notice comes in. Or they encounter a cash-flow problem one month and can't meet that last-second deadline.

Playing the bill-delaying game up to the edge of the safety margin is a dangerous practice and may one day get you into hot water with a creditor or a credit bureau.

These, then, are a number of ways that you can go into debt from a position of strength. By setting up an effective personal budget, developing a sound philosophy of debt and building a solid credit history, you'll be well on the road to a good credit rating. Furthermore, the route to a good credit rating involves putting restrictions on your reliance on credit, developing healthy borrowing habits and monitoring your credit status.

But this is just a first step in becoming a Power Borrower. Once you've laid the groundwork of healthy personal money management, the next step is to understand how the nation's tax laws may shape your borrowing strategy.

CHAPTER 4

Everything You Need to Know About Your Bank

For many people, banks seem to be formidable, even overwhelming institutions—especially when it's time to apply for a loan.

Some individuals worry, "There's no way I'll ever be able to qualify for the amount of money I need." Others moan, "Even if I get a loan, I'll end up paying exorbitant rates and going deeper and deeper into debt."

Banks and other lending institutions do sometimes seem more than ready to lend money, as long as the loan is made *on their terms.* In recent years, television advertising by banks, savings institutions, and personal finance companies has escalated to new levels: In 1982, for example, the price of such TV ads by banks and thrift institutions barely topped $150 million, while in 1987, the ad costs shot up toward $250 million.

What sorts of loans did these lenders typically promote? At one point, when the advertising was at a peak, the prime rate — or the loan interest banks charge their best customers

(i.e., top-rated corporations and governmental institutions)—
was at 8.75 percent. Also, the overnight loans banks made to
each other carried about 7-percent interest.

But consumer credit rates on such loan vehicles as credit
card purchases and unsecured overdraft privileges were
closer to 18 percent! In other words, if you had responded to
some of these promotions for many popular loan
arrangements, you would have found yourself paying nearly
10 percent more in interest than the banks' best institutional
customers.

No one who responds blindly or indiscriminately to such
advertising can hope to become a Power Borrower. Instead,
the Power Borrower must probe deeper into the banking scene
and learn how to make use of the most profitable answers to
some of these key questions:

- What are my borrowing options? Or to put this
another way, what types of lending institutions are
available to provide me with the most attractive
loan?

- How should I expect banks and other lending
institutions to deal with me as a prospective borrower—and make money from the business I give
them?

- What's the best way to get a good loan?

- How can I guard against a "hard sell" by banks
and other lenders?

- How can I get help with my borrowing from
governmental and consumer organizations?

Now, let's consider some answers to each of these
questions and see how this information can be applied to your
personal situation.

WHAT ARE YOUR BORROWING OPTIONS?

If you're in the market for a loan, you're certainly not limited to your local bank—though as we'll see later, the best deal may be available there. There are many alternative institutions that may be able to offer you attractive arrangements for loans, as well as for other banking-type services. So you should certainly be aware of the variety of possibilities before you make a final decision.

Here are some of the options you should consider:

Commercial banks

Of all the lenders, these financial institutions — of which Citibank and Bank of America are prime examples—have the widest range of consumer and business services. Recent deregulation in the banking industry has blurred many distinctions among commercial banks, savings and loan associations, and other financial institutions. In general, however, commercial banks offer the most comprehensive financial options.

In any event, if you choose a commercial bank for your business, including checking and savings arrangements, you should be sure that it's covered by the Federal Deposit Insurance Corporation (FDIC). This federal insurance protection will protect deposits of up to $100,000.

As for borrowing possibilities, commercial banks will offer you both secured and unsecured personal loans. A secured loan is one that is backed up by some sort of collateral, such as real estate, stocks, or a savings account. If the borrower fails to pay on the loan, the lender can then dip into the collateral to square the obligation. Typically, secured loans carry interest equal to the prime rate plus a relatively small extra percentage (recently, this extra percentage ranged from less than 1 percent to more than 2 percent over prime).

Unsecured loans, in contrast, are backed only by the borrower's personal signature and guarantee. If the borrower fails to pay on these loans, the bank may be forced to use legal channels to invade the borrower's other assets for payment.

Because unsecured loans are, by definition, less secure than secured loans, you can expect the interest rate for unsecured borrowers to be several percentage points higher. For example, in one recent survey, interest on secured loans ranged up to 12 percent, while interest on unsecured loans and lines of credit hit 18 percent in some banks. But remember: I'm citing figures that are available as this book is being written. Check the current figures when you actually decide to borrow.

Commercial banks will also lend money for a variety of other purposes, such as home improvements, first and second mortgages, and home equity credit lines.

Savings and Loan Associations

These are privately owned financial corporations that are chartered by either the state or federal government. If you have a savings account in one of these organizations, you should be sure that the money is protected by the Federal Savings and Loan Insurance Corporation (FSLIC). FSLIC covers savings accounts of up to $100,000.

Traditionally, these organizations existed for people who wanted to set up savings accounts or get loans for home mortgages. But since the deregulating legislation of recent years, savings and loans have expanded to provide extensive checking privileges, many kinds of consumer and commercial loans, and other services offered in the past by commercial banks.

Savings and loan associations still specialize in home mortgages. But they also offer a variety of secured and unsecured personal loans, car loans, and home improvement loans.

Credit Unions

Credit unions are cooperative organizations that usually make small personal loans available to members. Membership in these groups is typically limited to employees of a particular company or organization, or residents of a designated geographical area.

Credit unions should have charters under state law or be set up as federally approved organizations under the Credit Union Act of 1934. If you put money into a credit union savings account, you should be certain that the organization is insured by the National Credit Union Share Insurance Fund, which covers individual accounts up to $100,000. Also, the interest you receive on your savings may be higher than you can get at local banks and savings institutions.

There are also a number of loan possibilities with credit unions, including:

- Small secured personal loans, at about the same rates available with commercial banks or savings-and-loan associations
- Small unsecured personal loans
- A variety of loans on your residence, including first and second mortgages and home improvement loans (but home equity loans have not been as common with credit unions as with some other lenders)
- Car loans

In general, these borrowing opportunities involve about the same interest rates as are available with commercial banks and with savings and loans. But there is some variation among individual organizations — as much as 2 to 3 percent or more. So it's wise to shop around before you make a final commitment.

Personal finance companies
These organizations, which once focused on simple personal loans, now offer some additional financial service oppor-

tunities. The largest personal finance companies, for example, may offer savings accounts, such as certificates of deposit, that can be obtained through the mail. But if you want more complete savings, checking, and other banking services, you should go to traditional banks. The loans that personal finance companies offer include unsecured personal loans, first and second mortgages, and car loans. Secured personal loans are available from some companies, as are home equity credit lines. But these last two possibilities aren't as common with finance companies.

On the whole, interest rates for loans tend to be higher at finance companies—in part because the loan application requirements are less stringent than at banks. For example, one recent survey showed that rates at personal finance companies ranged up to 9 percent higher than those of banks on home mortgages; 6 percent higher on second mortgages; 16 percent higher on car loans; and 8 percent higher on unsecured personal loans.

Of course, if you shop around, you will probably be able to find finance company rates that are more competitive with banks and other lending institutions. In general, however, the Power Borrower should focus more on banks, savings and loans, and credit unions for his or her loan opportunities, except in cases of dire emergency.

I'm reminded here of one man whose apartment building was adjacent to a personal finance company. As is the case with all of us, he needed a regular supply of pocket cash for daily expenses. But his bank, which offered the services of an automated cash machine, was several blocks away, and often it seemed entirely in the wrong direction from the way he planned to travel. So he got into the habit of taking out small loans from the finance company when he was in a rush.

When this man had initially set up an unsecured credit line, he found the application procedure to be a breeze. The extra interest he was paying didn't particularly bother him because he had set up the credit line under the old tax law, when all interest payments were deductible.

Also, he liked the convenience of using the finance organization: Not only was the company next door to him, but also, there was never a line of other customers when he wanted to take out some money. To further minimize his costs, he kept his indebtedness to the finance company relatively low—never more than $300 to $400 at any given time.

But then, other financial pressures began to bear down on him. For several months, he found that he was unable to keep his indebtedness at the personal finance company as low as he had planned. Gradually, his loan balance crept up above $1,000, and he was paying interest at a rate of 25 percent a year.

Finally, at the end of the year, he discovered that this finance company interest, plus other interest he was paying on personal bank loans, had mounted up to more than $2,000 for the previous twelve-month period. And that was *interest alone*—he also had to repay principal. Furthermore, only a small percentage was deductible under the new tax laws.

Clearly, this man was *not* a Power Borrower. He had inadvertently slipped into bad personal credit habits, and far too much of his disposable income was going toward servicing his personal, noninvestment debts. Eventually, after a self-imposed period of financial austerity that lasted for nearly a year, this man got out from under his heavy debt load. But he could have avoided this problem in the first place if only he had been willing to walk that extra few blocks to his bank, rather than rely on the unsecured credit line at the nearby personal finance company.

Of course, I'm not suggesting that you will automatically avoid such debt problems just by avoiding personal finance companies. It's quite easy to fall into a similar trap by using overdraft privileges at a bank. Indebtedness through a bank's unsecured personal credit line, which may carry a relatively high interest rate, can do just as much damage to your finances. The only difference is that the damage done at the personal finance company will usually mount up more quickly!

In addition to the institutions just discussed, there are a number of others that offer important borrowing opportunities.

If you want a car loan, for instance, you may be better off going directly to a car dealer. Many times, extremely low-rate auto loans are available for buyers—loans that are more attractive than anything that can be obtained in banks or other lending institutions.

Also, retailing chains like K mart, J. C. Penney, and Sears, Roebuck are now offering a wide range of financial services, either directly or through bank outlets in their stores. These services include:

- Unsecured and secured personal loans
- Home improvement loans
- Car loans
- Home equity credit lines
- Other borrowing possibilities, such as mortgages, through banks with outlets in the chains

Some retailers have also established national credit card programs and savings opportunities like banks. On the whole, the borrowing rates are often competitive with banks and other lenders.

Brokerage firms are also another borrowing possibility. The tax benefits of borrowing through a margin account to pay for personal expenses aren't nearly as attractive now as in the past. But if you want to borrow to buy investments, a margin account is still a possibility. The major limitation is that after 1990, you won't be able to deduct interest that exceeds your net investment income.

But note: If you're not primarily concerned about tax deductions with your loan, you can still get a secured loan through a broker that is quite competitive with secured loans from other institutions. In fact, one recent study revealed that in some cases, secured brokerage loans charged over 1 percent less for interest than similar loans by banks, savings and loan associations, or credit unions.

This brief overview of your borrowing options suggests that a number of possibilities are available when you decide to take out a loan. But how should you go about making a choice between different banks, or between banks and other financial institutions? To answer this question, let's explore in more detail how banks and bankers operate, and how you can shop most effectively among them.

SOME TIPS FOR BORROWERS ON HOW BANKS WORK

This book is not the place to go into an extended explanation of the intricacies of the banking industry. But there are a few simple points about banks and related lending institutions that you should understand if you hope to become a Power Borrower. To this end, it's helpful for all borrowers to think in terms of three basic banking rules.

Rule 1: Your Banker Isn't God

Too often, prospective borrowers walk into the office of a banker or other lending officer with hat in hand, expecting that the banker knows everything and has all the power in the relationship. They look to him or her to dispense—virtually with the power of divine fiat—loan largesse, financial wisdom, and the final word about their borrowing potential.

But this attitude invests too much power in the hands of

the banker. The Power Borrower, in contrast, reserves considerable power in his own hands. He doesn't just go along with what the banker says or offers. Instead, he retains the final authority to make his own decisions about how and where he'll borrow money.

Rule 2: The Main Objective of Banks Is to Make Money

Banks are not charitable institutions. They exist to make a profit, and if they don't make a profit, their management will most likely be ousted by the shareholders. Or in the most serious cases, the bank will go out of business.

Another way to say this is that the bank's first responsibility is to its shareholders—to provide a reasonable return on each investment dollar. If the bank consistently fails to achieve a return (or make a profit), the stockholders may oust the management.

So when you apply for a loan at any lending institution, always keep in mind that the lender sitting across the table from you views you as part of his company's profit picture. He wants to be sure, first of all, that if he lends you money, you'll be likely to pay it back—and pay it back on time. Otherwise, his organization will lose money on you. Also, he wants you to pay as much interest for the use of that loan money as the current lending market will bear.

There are a number of channels that banks rely on to enhance their cash flow. One, as I've already indicated, is that they lend their money at the highest rates that the market will bear. The money that you as a borrower pay in interest for the use of the bank's money becomes part of the bank's overall income and profit.

The bank's interest rates are generally pegged to certain prevailing interest rates throughout the economy, including the rates paid on certain money instruments issued by the federal government. For example, the mortgage rates of a bank will generally be tied to the rates of the six-month treasury bills.

So, if the six-month treasury bill rate is 6 percent, one bank may offer mortgage rates of 6 percent plus a "spread" of, say, an additional 3 percent, for a total mortgage rate of 9 percent. Another bank may offer a mortgage at the treasury rate plus a 2.5 percent spread, for a total mortgage rate of 8.5 percent.

This same sort of variation in interest rates occurs with other types of loans, such as secured and unsecured personal loans and auto loans. For example, in one recent report, the rate for an unsecured line of credit at a variety of the nation's banks varied from 14 percent to 18 percent. In fixing these rates, the banks generally look to the prevailing prime rate (the interest rate they charge their best institutional customers). Then, they add as many percentage points as they feel the current market will bear to loans of borrowers other than their top-rated institutional customers. The additional percentage points also reflect the greater risk of lending to an individual than to a top-rated institution.

As you can see, there is some leeway that a bank's management has in setting interest rates, so it pays you to shop around for the best borrowing deal. Clearly, any given bank will probably try to push its interest rates to the upper limit. But that doesn't mean that you, as a borrower, have to accept that upper limit if you can find a lower rate elsewhere. These banks are in competition with one another as they try to get your business, and so your objective should be to find the one that has the most attractive deal.

Banks invest the money that comes in to them as deposits in savings and checking accounts, individual retirement plans (IRAs), Keogh plans, and other such accounts. They try to invest this money at higher rates than they are paying to their customers, and the difference, once again, becomes part of their income and profit picture.

Another way that banks make money from individual customers is through their credit card operations. The lending institutions issue national credit cards, like Visa or Master-

Card, to their customers. Then, they receive money from their customers through these cards in a number of ways.

First, they charge an annual fee, which may range from about $15 to $50. Then, they collect regular interest from the millions of customers—about two thirds of all cardholders—who fail to pay off their credit card charges completely each month. These customers, who make use of the "revolving-credit" feature of their cards, pay only part of the balance. Then, under the terms of the credit card agreement, the bank can charge interest on the remaining portion of the balance. This interest is often the highest interest rate that banks charge for any of their lending services!

Finally, banks charge penalty fees for customers who fail to pay off the minimum balance by the time required under the card agreement.

These are some of the major ways that the nation's banks may make money from you if you've become involved in one or more of their lending opportunities. Of course, there are many other ways that banks make money, such as through fees they charge for various financial services they render. But the major lessons for you, as a borrower, can be derived from some simple responses to the above ways that we've seen banks make money from individual customers.

   • *Lesson 1:* Don't accept the first loan interest rate that is offered to you. You know these rates vary, so shop around!

   • *Lesson 2:* Check the terms of any credit card agreement that you are considering before you sign it, and go for the card that offers the best interest rates and other features that will minimize your costs. (For more on these matters, see the following chapter.)

   • *Lesson 3:* Pay up your credit card bills when they are due. Don't become a "revolver" by allowing a

balance, on which the bank can charge interest, to
carry over from month to month. (Again, see the
more detailed discussion on this and related points
in the following chapter.)

Rule 3: Expect Your Banker to Be a Fair but Tough Lender

At a regular review meeting in one of the nation's major
banks, one officer took the floor and said, "I have this great list
we can mail out to bring in new customers. It's a list of
borrowers who are within about six months of paying off their
loans with personal finance companies. What do you say we
offer them our lower interest rates over a longer term—say a
year to eighteen months?"

A major idea behind this proposal was that some of the
borrowers on that list would continue indefinitely as the
bank's customers and would make ongoing use of the bank's
highest-priced loan offerings.

To be sure, the loan rates that the bank was offering were
considerably less than those of the personal finance company.
In this case, the finance company rate that the borrowers on
the list were paying was about 23 percent, while the bank rate
was closer to 18 percent. But still, the proposal seemed
designed to keep the customers indefinitely in the position of
borrowers, rather than to help them continue toward their
goal of becoming debt-free. And that prospect bothered some
of the other banking officials around the table.

"This concept bothers me," one of the other bankers
objected. "What do you plan to call this — our 'Statue of
Liberty list'? In other words, we'll take your 'poor and
downtrodden' and *keep* them 'poor and downtrodden'?"

"No, no, this is a legitimate idea," the proponent argued.
"We'd spell out all the terms of the new borrowing agreement.
We'd say they've demonstrated that they are good credit risks,
and now we're going to reward them for their achievements."

But this argument didn't convince the majority of those
present. Others quickly jumped on the consumer-oriented

bandwagon: "Oh come on!" one of the man's colleagues
responded. "These people are within just a few months of one
of the proud accomplishments of their lifetimes. Yet you're
going to deny them that satisfaction. You're suggesting that
we tempt them with an ongoing debt load by sweetening the
burden with a slightly lower interest rate."

After several minutes of discussion, the idea was rejected,
but I find the discussion of this issue to be instructive about
how some bankers may think. In some institutions, this idea
might have immediately been accepted by everyone, and put
into effect. But this bank, which was more sensitive to
consumer interests and possible damage to its image in the
community, chose to back off.

The main point to keep in mind here is that bankers are
human beings who vary greatly in their attitudes toward their
customers. Some will be extremely aggressive in bringing in
new accounts, even if that means encouraging the new
customers to go into debt further than they should.

Of course, no banker wants to push a customer over the
edge so that he or she is unable to pay back his loans. All banks
assume that some loans—amounting to about 2 to 3 percent of
the credit balances outstanding on credit cards—will be lost.
But they don't look for trouble from a customer, and their loan
applications are designed to screen out those people who are
bad risks. Still, the pressure to increase business causes some
lenders to put more emphasis on making money in the short
term from a customer than helping that customer become a
long-term, financially solid client.

On the whole, however, I've found that the large majority
of bankers are fair-minded and sensitive to consumer issues,
especially when they get involved with individual customers.
One owner of a small business told me that he had received
better practical advice and more personal attention from his
banker than from anyone else.

"He was great at coming up with little maxims that stuck
with me in the early years of my business," this man said.

"For example, at the very outset, as I was applying for a small loan, he told me, 'The first thing every person starting a new business should do is to hire two key people to advise him: a good accountant, and a good lawyer.' "

The entrepreneur took this advice, and he reported later that he had saved thousands of dollars through the tax strategies formulated by his accountant and the tight contracts drawn up by his attorney.

You can't expect your banker or other lender to forget his obligations to the organization that employs him and put all his efforts into giving you financial breaks. Any good banker will be reasonably tough with a customer in that he will try to make sure the customer is a good risk before he recommends that the person be given a loan. After all, if the customer turns out to be a bad risk—and either is a chronic late payer or fails to pay at all—the loan officer is the one who has to answer for the problem.

But after a solid lender-borrower relationship has been established and nurtured over a period of time, the real value of having a good banker in your corner when you need a loan or some other financial service becomes apparent.

But before such a relationship can be established, it's necessary first for you, the prospective borrower, to find the best possible place to take out your loan. Yet how do you find the right bank or other lending institution? And once you've found a desirable lender, how do you get him or her to respond positively to your application?

A BRIEF GUIDE TO GETTING A GOOD LOAN

From many of the points we've already discussed, you should already have a fairly good idea about what you have to do to get a good loan. But now, let me summarize some of these points, and add some practical new information, in the form of several steps.

Step 1: Establish a personal position
of strength as a borrower

For details on this step, refer back to the strengths described in Chapter 2. In brief, these include:

- Having a sound personal budget
- Having a sound philosophy of debt
- Having a solid credit history—which will open the door to a good credit rating

Anyone who wants to be in the most powerful position to get an attractive loan agreement must be on solid ground with each of these borrowing strengths.

Step 2: Identify the precise objective
for which you want the loan or credit line

Too often, I run into people who want a credit line or overdraft privilege for reasons like these:

- "To cover me just in case I overspend one month."
- "To act as a buffer because too often I bounce checks."
- "To provide a safety net if I should run into financial problems." Or:
- "To provide cash for last-minute vacation needs or other personal expenses."

These reasons for credit aren't really sufficient to justify setting up a credit line or taking out a loan because they tend to reflect a lack of personal financial planning. Think about it for a moment: If you have a well-thought-out family or personal budget, you won't overspend. If you keep track of your expenses and the state of your checking account, you won't bounce checks.

Furthermore, the best safety net for personal financial problems is not a credit line. Rather, it's a savings account that has been accumulated over time for vacations, unexpected expense overruns, or the contingencies of the proverbial "rainy day."

Also, as an alternative for an overdraft arrangement to guard against bounced checks, some banks will link your savings accounts to your checking account. In this way, if a check deposited to your account hasn't cleared and you draw on it, the bank won't bounce your check. Instead, they put a hold against a portion of your savings account until the deposited check clears.

Other valid objectives for a loan or credit line might include some specific goals as these:

- A mortgage to buy a home, condominium, or cooperative apartment
- A personal credit line or margin account with a broker to use for the purchase of personal investments
- A credit line that can be used periodically to put money into a business you may own
- A loan to buy an automobile
- A loan to help pay for your child's education

The main idea here is to be completely clear in your own mind what you want to use the loan for. Then, be disciplined enough to limit your use of the money only for that purpose.

Step 3: Check first with your local bank

In general, I always advise my clients first to ask their local banker, with whom they do most of their regular banking business, what kind of a deal he can offer them for a loan.

Sometimes, if you're a customer who maintains what bankers may call "mundane balances" (or minimal deposits in the bank), you won't get any break. But if you're more of a "priority customer" who keeps fairly substantial balances, uses credit lines, and pays on time, you will probably qualify for some sort of preferential treatment.

To test whether good customers could indeed expect preference over noncustomers, I checked with five banks near me in Manhattan to see what kinds of rates I could get on two different types of loans—unsecured personal loans and auto loans. The difference between the treatment of customers and noncustomers was significant.

Noncustomers at these banks were being offered an interest range on three-year personal loans of 14 percent to 16.5 percent. In contrast, customers could receive a range of 12.9 percent to 14.5 percent.

As for the auto loans, noncustomers were getting an interest range of 12 to 13 percent on a two- to five-year car loan. Customers, however, were being offered a much more attractive 10 to 11 percent.

A number of banks even advertise in their brochures that their customers can qualify for reduced loan rates. One major American bank says in one of its handouts that the bank's loans give customers "a chance to qualify for significant savings on a wide variety of loan programs."

According to this particular bank, these lower-rate loans can be used for home improvements, the purchase of a car or boat, or a "splurge on that special luxury you've put off too long." (I don't recommend, however, that you make this last objective part of your personal borrowing program!)

The point is that it's wise to check with your local bank first—and only then proceed with the next step.

Step 4: Shop around

I've mentioned that I had checked with five banks in my area to see what their rates were on two different types of loans. That's precisely the approach you should take when you find yourself in the market for a loan.

It's important to look upon a loan as just another product or service that is being offered to you as a consumer. Remember: There are loans, and there are loans—and while they may all put money into your pocket, the cost of that money and the services that accompany it may vary greatly.

Consider once more my experience with those five banks. As you can see, if you were a noncustomer looking for an unsecured personal loan, you could have paid a difference of 2.5 percent in annual interest, depending on which bank you chose. On a $10,000 loan, that would amount to a $250 a year difference in interest — or $750 over the three-year life of the loan. Obviously, the difference in the cost of borrowing money can be considerable, even in one neighborhood.

Step 5: Evaluate every detail of any
loan agreement that is offered to you

You should feel free to ask the loan officers of various banks direct, detailed questions about the meaning of the applications and agreements they are showing you for the loan.

If you feel you're not getting straight or adequate answers, ask to see a supervisor. This can be done in a tactful way, such as, "I really need to know the answer to this question. Should we check with someone else here to get the specifics?"

The types of questions you should ask a loan officer include these:

- I need ____ dollars—will you be able to provide a loan in that amount? If not, how much can I borrow from you? (Generally speaking, the minimum amount you can borrow as an unsecured personal loan is $500 and the maximum is $25,000.)

- What interest rate are you charging?

- Are there any ways to get a lower rate (e.g., as a bank customer, by having the loan payments deducted automatically from my bank account, etc.)?

Note: Some banks will provide you with additional savings if you use their automatic deduction option, but others won't. So you'll have to ascertain their precise policy before you make your decision on this issue.

If you choose to have your loan payments deducted from your checking account, that arrangement will make it more certain that you won't miss a payment. But it's important to ascertain as well as you can how reliable the system is.

Some banks have extremely good payment deduction systems, but others may make periodic mistakes. In other words, they'll take the same payment out twice, or they'll deduct the wrong amount. If you don't keep close track of your bank account, you could find that you're bouncing checks when you believed, quite justifiably, that you had plenty of money available in your account.

So I would ask the lending officer directly, "Tell me, is this system really reliable? Have you ever encountered any mistakes with it?" More often than not, you'll get a straightforward, truthful answer and you can make your decision based on the lender's response. Or if you know other customers who have used the system, you may be able to get information from them about whether or not you should try it.

As I've said, many banks won't offer you a better interest rate just because you have your payments deducted automatically. So you'll have to do some research and compile a list of all the advantages and disadvantages on this issue before you make a final decision.

• What is the exact total dollar amount I'll have to pay back on the loan, including principal and interest?

• How long will I have to pay the loan back?

• Is the interest rate fixed, or is it variable? If it's variable, is there a ceiling on the maximum amount of interest I may have to pay? Is there a floor on the minimum?

• Is there a "balloon payment" at the end of the loan, which will require me to make one large, final lump-sum payment? If so, what are the consequences if I'm not able to come up with all the money for that payment when it's due?

Note: Balloon payments are usually set up to keep the initial loan payments low during a period when the person's income or ability to repay is expected to be relatively low. Then, the large final payment is supposedly scheduled at a time when the individual's income or repayment ability is higher. Unfortunately, however, one's income or repayment ability doesn't always increase as expected.

• Is there a grace period during which I can wait before I have to make my first payment on the loan? If so, how long is it?

• What is the length of time over which I must pay back the loan?

• If I pay back the loan early, how much, if anything can I save on interest?

• If I'm late in making a payment, will I be hit with a penalty? If so, how much will it be?

• Can I pay a month in advance on my loan in case I'm going to be out of the country or otherwise unavailable?

• Can I take out insurance to cover the loan in case I die before it's paid off? How much will this insurance cost?

Note: It's often advisable to take out such insurance if you're the head of a household and your spouse has cosigned the loan and would become liable in the event of your death.

Obviously, there are many other questions that you might ask a loan officer at a bank or other lending institution. But these should give you an idea about some of the areas that you should think about before you go in for your interview.

In any discussion with a banker, it's helpful to have a list of questions written out in front of you. Then, jot down the lender's answers and check off each question when he or she has responded in a way that satisfies you.

Above all, keep a topic or point of discussion "on the table" with the banker until you understand it thoroughly. In this regard, it's usually helpful to evaluate a loan both in terms of the interest percentage being offered, and also the dollar amounts you'll have to repay.

Step 6: Sidestep the hard sell!

As we've already seen, banks like other businesses have become heavily involved in doing hard-hitting advertising in the broadcast and print media. But if you get into the habit of asking probing, direct questions—and sticking with those questions until you get satisfactory answers—you'll find you can usually reduce the pressure that causes many people to succumb to the hard sell.

For example, many lenders offer very low "come-on" rates in their advertising. But then, after a year or so, their rates may shoot up well above what other lenders are charging. By simply asking, "What are the rates over the entire life of the loan?" you'll be well on your way toward avoiding the trap of these advertising pitches.

But it's not always easy to take the cautious, conservative road when you're offered a swinging vacation, a flashy cabin cruiser, or a mortgage for a supposedly luxurious dream house. One set of bank ads recently suggested that loans could be used for a very expensive wedding for your child, an adventurous trip to the Arctic, or commuting by helicopter to and from work! Many people would love to have these luxuries, and some may actually believe they *can* have them—if they listen uncritically to the hard-selling lender, rather than to the quiet, inner voice of their own better judgment.

Some lenders are now also relying on the telephone to set up loans in an effort to overcome the traditionally forbidding experience of walking into a banker's office. One company has promised over-the-phone rejection or approval of personal loans within a half hour. Also, they provide potential customers with an 800 toll-free number sticker that they can affix to their phones for easier access to the lender.

These tactics, presented as benefits, are intended to provide the customer with convenience and encouragement to make a quick decision. For Power Borrowers, they may be

true benefits. For the Weak Borrower, however, they are
invitations to trouble. If you're not sure which type of
borrower you are, be more cautious and apply in person for a
loan. In this way, you can explore in more detail the questions
I've suggested throughout this chapter.

THE POWER BORROWER AS A
CONSUMMATE BANKING CONSUMER

As a borrower, you're a consumer. You're paying for an
important service—the use of a lender's money. So you should
be sure that you know your rights and are fully protected
under the law. That way, you'll be more likely to get the most
for your money.

To achieve this objective, most borrowers I counsel find
it extremely helpful to make use of consumer-oriented literature and advice from organizations in their area that focus on
the practices of lending institutions. These agencies often
publish comparative rate schedules at different banks and
other lending institutions. Also, they may provide other
insights that will help you make intelligent borrowing decisions.

To gain access to this information, you'll have to contact
various state and federal banking agencies that oversee lending
operations where you live. Also, you may find that private
consumer groups can be of considerable help. Here are a few
examples of the types of organizations that you may want to
check:

- For those banks that have "National" or "N.A."
(National Association) in their title, write or
call your local regional administrator of national
banks, or:

Regional Administrator of National Banks
1211 Avenue of the Americas, Suite 4250
New York, New York 10036
(212) 944-3491 or 3495

• For savings banks or savings and loan associations with the word "Federal" in their name, or with the initials FSB (Federal Savings Bank), FSA (Federal Savings Association), FA (Federal Association), or FSLA (Federal Savings and Loan Association), write or call:

Federal Home Loan Bank
One World Trade Center
New York, New York 10048
(212) 912-4600 or 4637

• For credit unions with the word "Federal" in their title, contact:

National Credit Union Administration Regional Administrator
State Street South Building, Room 3E
441 Steward Street
Boston, Massachusetts 02116
(617) 223-6807

• Write to your state consumer protection board for information on your rights as a bank customer.

• Write to your state banking department, consumer services division, for information on state-licensed banks.

• For information on credit reporting companies, lending practices, debt collection, or loan advertising, write:

Federal Trade Commission
Fair Credit Reporting Section

26 Federal Plaza—22nd Floor
New York, New York 10278

These are just a few of the possibilities. But the more you
investigate and learn about how your banks and other lending
institutions work, the better consumer you'll be—and the
more money you'll save.

CHAPTER 5

Winning at Cards

"Plastic money"—including credit cards, debit cards, bank cards, and other synthetic cash substitutes—has proliferated in recent years.

Banks issue two types of cards: One gives you access to your checking account, savings, and perhaps a credit line at the bank. The other—a MasterCard or Visa—can provide cash advances from your credit card account. Also, with this second type, you can just forget about using cash and buy the item or service directly with the plastic.

The prevalence of these cards has changed the way we conduct our daily lives and pursue our business interests. Consider for a moment the magnitude of the credit card phenomenon:

- Approximately 106 million people in America use some sort of credit card—including cards issued by banks, department stores, fuel companies, and other organizations. Furthermore, each of these people holds an average of eight cards!

- Banks are the pillars of the credit card business: More than eighty million Americans age eighteen and older have at least one bank credit card, according to the *Bank Credit Card Observer*. Nearly forty million have two or more cards.

• College graduates spend on average nearly $400 a month by credit card, according to the Federal Reserve Board. Those with some college spend an average of about $160 monthly, and high school graduates spend more than $80 a month.

• According to the Federal Reserve Board, between 1984 and 1986 total monthly credit card charges rose more than 27 percent.

• Surveys of MasterCard and other credit card holders show that about two thirds of those who use their cards *don't* pay their bills in full each month. That is, they are "revolvers" who make partial payments and finance the balance by carrying the balance of their bills as interest-bearing loans.

Obviously, plastic money has permeated our society. But before we go any further with this discussion, it's important to distinguish between some of the major types of plastic.

First of all, when I refer to credit cards, I'm *not* talking about cards issued by banks that are designed only to be used in automated teller machines (ATMs). Of course, if you have a card of this type that gives you access to an overdraft privilege on your checking account—so that you can take out more money than you have on deposit as a loan—then it's arguable that your ATM card is a kind of credit card. But the classic credit card is usually regarded as a vehicle basically different from these bank cards. The reason? With a credit card, you can purchase goods and services directly.

Also, credit cards must be distinguished from the so-called *debit cards*. A debit card usually involves an immediate deduction from your checking account or brokerage account when you make a purchase. In many ways, using a debit card is much like writing a check—except that you'll lose the "float" you get from writing a check. *Note:* In this context, the term "float" refers to the delay between the time you write a check and the time at which the amount of the check is charged against your bank account.

In contrast, with a credit card, you often have three or four weeks to make a payment for your purchases. The credit card payment usually is due after a designated "grace period" of twenty to thirty days following the date when the bill for your purchase was issued. During this grace period, no interest accrues on the payment due for the purchase. After the grace period expires, you're required to pay interest on the unpaid balance in your credit card account.

Those who pay their bills within the grace period, and thus incur no interest charges, are known as "nonrevolvers." Those who pay only part of their bills and allow the balance to carry over to the next accounting period, so that they are required to pay interest, are called "revolvers."

Some cards—notably the American Express green and platinum cards, Diners Club, and Carte Blanche—are frequently referred to as "charge cards" or "travel and entertainment cards" instead of credit cards. Purchases on these cards become due in full immediately upon receipt of the bill, and do not allow for revolving credit.

I, however, lump these so-called charge cards in with regular credit cards for a couple of reasons:

• Payment for purchases made with charge cards really isn't due immediately upon receipt. These companies traditionally allow a period of time that often extends beyond regular credit card grace periods before they begin to send dunning notices to cardholders. American Express, for example, will allow forty-five days or even longer for payment before they impose a penalty or suspend privileges. By most standards, this extended grace period would be regarded as a form of credit.

- Many of the charge cards allow revolving-credit arrangements for certain purchases (e.g., airline tickets) or upon special application to the company.

But even after we narrow down and define more precisely the concept of the credit card, a tough question remains: How do you go about choosing the best credit card for your personal needs?

HOW TO CHOOSE AND USE
A PERSONAL CREDIT CARD

Margaret, a rather successful single professional woman in her thirties, found just after the Christmas holidays one year that she was burdened by excessive debt—most of which arose from her credit card purchases.

Like many other people in our society, she held several credit cards, but in many ways, Margaret had gone overboard: She actively used a MasterCard, Visa, American Express, Diners Club, Discover, three department store cards, and two gasoline company cards. Ten pieces of plastic money in all—with a total credit line on the cards alone that exceeded $30,000! Furthermore, Margaret had unfortunately made so many purchases on these cards that her total outstanding balances reached more than $25,000. A Weak Borrower by almost any definition!

In some respects, however, Margaret was an unusual Weak Borrower, because she hadn't really abused her other credit privileges. She owned a moderately priced automobile that was almost fully paid off. Also, even though she had access to unsecured credit lines at her bank that totaled more than $20,000, she only owed $1,000 on them. In addition, she owned a condominium that was well within the means of her $45,000 annual salary.

Margaret's problem didn't lie so much in these other borrowing areas as it did in her credit cards. She was a chronic impulse buyer who couldn't seem to walk past a clothing store, electronics outlet, or gift shop without making a purchase.

"It's so painless just to go in, select an item, and put one of my credit cards on the counter for payment," she said. "But then the pain arrives with a vengeance when I get those bills!"

The solution for Margaret was stiff: Destroy all her credit cards but one, her Visa card. The reason for retaining the Visa card is that car rental agencies require a credit card when you rent, or else you must pay a rather large deposit. In some cases, you may not be able to rent a car at all without a credit card! I suggested Visa because the one she carried had an annual fee that was less than that for MasterCard and the other national cards.

Margaret had to embark on a cash-only budget and gradually, over a period of slightly more than a year, pay off all her outstanding credit card debts. Then, when she had "cleared the decks" of her personal finances, she would be in a position to reevaluate whether she wanted to return gradually to more sensible credit card usage.

There were several reasons why I suggested such drastic measures. In the first place, Margaret was on the verge of financial disaster because of the extent to which she had gone into debt. If she had incurred just a few more obligations, she would have discovered that she was unable to make ends meet on her income.

Also, it became evident after one or two conversations that she was a hard-core impulse buyer. She simply lacked the willpower to say no to the temptation to buy an attractive suit, or a new gimmick for her stereo, or the latest attachment for her camera. Also, she had accumulated a laundry list of unnecessary services offered by the credit card companies: excessive amounts of term life insurance and flight insurance, a discount shopping service, and an automobile road service, just to name a few.

So it was essential that for a time, she back off completely from the use of credit. Getting accustomed to buying goods and services by cash—and to the relief of not being deep in debt—was essential for her future financial health. When Margaret learned how to manage her personal finances more wisely, she would be in a better position to move from the position of Weak Borrower to Power Borrower.

Margaret had entirely too many credit cards for any normal person's needs. The privileges provided by many of them overlapped with those of other cards she held. And they were expensive: Purchases aside, when we added up only the annual fees charged by the cards, we found she was paying almost $200 a year just for the right to carry those pieces of plastic around in her pocket!

Putting the tendency to overspend aside for a moment, I also had another reason for her to cut back on cards: With so many in her possession, she ran the personal risk of significant loss through theft. Purse snatchers use credit cards immediately.

Margaret is still paying off her credit card debts, but the prognosis for her future financial health is good. In fact, I suspect that she will eventually be able to return to some form of wise credit card use. Still, with her history of impulse purchasing, she'll always be one of those people who is potentially vulnerable to credit abuse.

This woman's experience provides us not only with a warning about the dangers of credit cards, but also with an introduction to some of the basic principles that everyone should follow in selecting and using a card. I prefer to deal with these principles in the form of a series of questions, which I always ask myself—and encourage others to ask—before applying for, accepting, or renewing a credit card.

Question 1: Why do I need the card? Whether you already have several cards or are considering getting your first one, it's a good idea to set aside a few minutes and ask yourself, "Do I really need a credit card?" In our society, that may seem to be a rather silly question because after all, most people have plastic money of some sort. But most people have never thought seriously about why they have cards or how they should use them. It's only by putting such a question to yourself that you can begin to sort through the purposes for which you hold and use your cards.

Some of the reasons that people have mentioned to me for having a credit card include the following:

- *Convenience*

  "I don't like to carry a lot of cash around with me."

  "I hate to have to rely on checkbooks and identification cards—which some places won't even accept."

  "I shop regularly at certain establishments, and my credit card is an easy way to buy and get discounts at these stores."

  "My card offers easy access to low-cost life insurance and other benefits."

  "It's nearly impossible to rent a car without a credit card—and I rent a lot of cars when I travel."

  "Sometimes I forget to carry cash with me."

- *Protection*

  "I often worry that if I carry a lot of cash around with me, I'll get mugged or lose it."

  "I'm afraid I may run short of money when I'm out with friends or away or on a trip."

- *Better accounting*

  "I like to get a statement every month showing where my money is going."

  "I manage my personal budget better when I get regular receipts and invoices."

- *Credit rating*
"I plan to borrow periodically in the future, and I want to be sure that I have a good track record as a borrower so that I can qualify for a bank loan."

- *Prestige*
"It looks classier to pull out a gold card than it does to sort through a lot of cash."

- *Available credit*
"My cash flow is unpredictable, and I like to know that I have credit readily available when I need it."

Each of the above reasons has something to commend it, though the first four certainly should carry more weight than the last two for the person who aspires to become a Power Borrower. In any case, none of these justifications for holding a credit card is inherently right or wrong.

The main point to keep in mind in mulling over this question is what *your* reasons are—and whether or not you feel they carry sufficient weight to warrant your holding a card. If you really can't come up with a solid reason, then perhaps you'd be better off not having one more card—or not having a credit card at all!

Question 2: How many cards do I need? Credit cards can certainly be a great convenience, but it's possible to get too much of a good thing. Consider the situation we just discussed that was faced by Margaret. With her ten credit cards, she was paying almost $200 in annual fees. Yet the cost wasn't necessary because the services and privileges offered by many of the cards she held overlapped.

More and more, the distinctions are disappearing among "travel and entertainment" charge cards like American Express, bank cards like MasterCard or Visa, and various other forms of plastic money, such as department store cards. Recently, for example, Visa and MasterCard made inroads into some of the country's major department stores. In the past, these stores had only recognized their own store card-holders or certain charge cards like American Express. As a result of such changes, the advantages of one card over another have begun to blur, and in many cases, it has become possible and even preferable for consumers to reduce the number of cards they hold.

In practical terms, how should you decide on the number of cards that's best for you?

Obviously, to figure out how many cards you need, you can't do an establishment-by-establishment evaluation of each of your credit cards. But it is possible to keep your eyes open during the course of a month and take some notes on where you typically use your cards. If you find that you can get by on one or two rather than four or five or more, then I'd advise you to pick the one or two that seem best for your purposes and get rid of the others.

Also, there's a new thrust among banks to acquire more MasterCard and Visa accounts. They are forming relation-ships with "affinity groups"—such as AAA (American Automobile Association), AARP (American Association for Retired People), various universities, and other institutions.

The cards issued through these arrangements are often much like regular MasterCards and Visa cards—though some-times, there are decided differences, such as the elimination of the grace period for payment purposes. Also, these affinity cards show the name of the organization on the application, and the organization benefits financially from the arrange-ment.

But remember: It's important to charge with your head, not your heart! Just because old State U makes money every time you use its card, that doesn't mean you should go out on a spending spree. A Power Borrower would be more likely to donate to the annual fund drive and get a charitable deduction, than to contribute "indirectly" at a higher cost.

Question 3: What is the annual fee for the card? Most credit cards require holders to pay an annual fee—the lowest being $20, and the most expensive, $55 or more. As we've already seen, the cost of the card begins with the annual fee. If you can choose a card with a relatively low annual fee, you're already ahead of the game.

In fact, most experts in this field acknowledge that most credit card holders are more "fee-sensitive" than "interest-rate-sensitive." In other words, if the fee is low, the consumer is more likely to sign up for that card than for a card with a higher fee—regardless of the annual interest charged for those with a revolving balance.

The fee is an important factor to consider—perhaps the most important if you're sure you're going to be a "nonre-volver" (a person who pays off his balance each month). But many financial counselors believe that for most people, who may at one time or another fail to pay off their entire credit card balance when it comes due, the interest rate should be a prime consideration in choosing a credit card.

Question 4: What is the annual interest rate for unpaid balances on the card? As you know, I don't recommend that anyone get into the habit of using a revolving credit card, whereby they pay off only a portion of the amount due and then incur interest on the balance. With the increasingly restricted ability to write off personal interest deductions on income tax returns, paying interest on credit cards can only weaken you financially. It's difficult if not impossible to be a regular revolver and a Power Borrower at the same time.

Sometimes, however, it may be necessary or unavoidable to allow part of a credit card balance to move over to the next payment period. For example, you may be out of town on an extended business trip or vacation after the bill comes due and after any grace period has elapsed. In those cases, it's comforting to know that you have access to the lowest possible interest rate—though these days, it does take some shopping and analysis to get the best percentage arrangement.

In recent years, interest rates on outstanding credit card balances have varied considerably at various banks around the country. They have ranged from less than 11 percent to nearly 20 percent—quite a difference, which potentially can mean the loss of large amounts of money for those who revolve hefty balances.

On the whole, however, the larger banks such as Bank of America and Citibank have kept their rates high, near the top of the interest rate structure. One recent study reported that the ten top bank issuers of credit cards, which account for about 34 percent of all the outstanding cards, had an average annual interest rate of 19.19 percent.

Unfortunately, a huge number of cardholders don't seem to pay much attention to the interest rates they're paying on their credit cards. According to a survey by the *American Banker*, almost 40 percent of the credit card holders who were polled didn't know the interest rate they were being charged on their most frequently used card!

Still, the consumer who looks around can find much lower rates than the average. At the same time, it's important to check out all the terms of those rates before signing up for them. Here are a few points to keep in mind:

- Some of the lower rates may only be offered for *limited periods* of time, such as six months.

- In a number of cases, lower rates are offered at the expense of reducing or limiting other credit card benefits, such as the grace period. One bank in Missouri, for example, lowered its rate to 10 percent on balances above $1,000, but it also eliminated the grace period.

- Some banks establish interest rates according to borrowing *tiers:* Customers who maintain revolving balances above certain levels—such as $1,000, $2,000, $3,000, and $4,000—become eligible for progressively lower interest rates. One New Jersey bank with this particular tier system charged customers who owed less than $1,000 18.8 percent. But the percentage dropped steadily until those with balances over $4,000 only had to pay 14.8 percent interest.

At first glance, this sort of tier arrangement may seem to be a good deal. But remember: Even though you may be paying lower interest rates at those higher balances, you're also paying much more money in total interest. Even more serious, you're moving far into debt and definitely not positioning yourself as a Power Borrower. And remember: If you take one year to pay off $1,000 on a card that charges interest at an annual percentage rate of 18.8 percent, you are really paying $1,188 for that item.

• An increasing number of banks are offering *variable* interest rates. American Express's new Optima card is priced similarly, with rates adjusted according to fluctuations in the prime rate.

The rates for both the bank credit cards and other companies' cards are typically set several points above the prime rate. So, if prime is 9 percent, a bank or other lending institution may add an extra 6 percent for a total interest rate of 15 percent. In other cases, the rate on a bank credit card may be based on the current rate of its three-month certificate of deposit, or on the six-month treasury bill rate. An extra percentage such as 6 percent is always added to these base rates.

Would a variable-rate credit card be right for you?

In recent years, these cards have been especially attractive because they have charged lower interest rates than fixed-rate cards. At the same time, there are trade-offs: For one thing, they typically have higher annual fees than other cards. As a result, if you're a nonrevolving credit card user, you will probably find that the higher annual fees on the variable-rate cards make them less attractive.

Also, if you do decide to go the variable-rate route, you'll have to keep a close watch on how the interest rates on your card fluctuate in comparison with fixed-rate cards. It could be that at some future time, your variable-rate arrangement will become more expensive than the fixed-rate cards.

So you'll have to sit down and figure out whether the total costs on a variable-rate credit card add up to an advantage of disadvantage for you.

• Finally, it's important to understand exactly how your credit card interest rate is calculated.

Cards may take different approaches to their minimum payment requirements, which can have an impact on the amount of interest you pay. Some minimum payments may be based on a thirty-six-month payoff period, while others may be based on a sixty-month payoff period. If your card company has chosen the longer period, you'll find you're paying more in interest if you continue to make the minimum payments.

Also, the amount of interest you pay may be influenced by the way your credit card company applies any partial payments you make. Assume, for instance, that you owe $300—$150 for some item you bought in a department store, and $150 for a cash advance. If the company first pays off your cash advance and then pays off the department store purchase, you may end up paying more in interest because the interest rate may be higher for the department store purchases. So it's wise to find out from your credit card agreement or from a representative of the company exactly how your payments are apportioned between the cash advance and the department store purchases.

Many times, the credit card interest rates are different from purchase and cash advances. Sometimes, the rate for cash advances is higher than for purchases; sometimes it's lower; and sometimes it's the same. So you should check your credit card agreement closely to see what the rules are. If you can't find the answer in the contract, call the 800 number listed on your bill or other literature to get the information.

Clearly, the question of credit card interest is complex, and quite frankly, I'd advise you to discipline yourself so that you don't have to get into this question at all. If you operate consistently as a Power Borrower, you'll pay off your credit card bills as they come due, without incurring any interest charges.

Question 5: Are there any late payment charges or other special fees required by the card? With some cards, if you are late making a payment, there is a late charge that is added to the regular interest rate. For example, under current practice, you get slapped with a $10 late fee if your MasterCard payment is sixty days late, and the fee may be $10 to $15 if a Visa payment is late.

Also, many credit cards include an extra charge every time a holder uses the card to get a cash advance. Some cards now offer cardholders the ability to transfer cash to a third party. To do this, the cardholder calls a toll-free number to trigger the transaction. But again, the fees can accumulate.

There would be a fee for transferring the money and also a daily finance charge, both on the amount transferred and also on the fee that has been charged!

For example, if you transfer $250 to a third party, you'd typically have to pay $22 for the privilege of making the transfer. In addition, with many banks, you'd pay more than 19-percent interest on the $250 *and* on the $22 fee.

It may be that you don't plan to use your card for any of these purposes. But if there's a chance you might, it will pay for you to figure out the different costs of the cards you're considering.

Question 6: Does the card provide for a "grace period"? A grace period is a stated amount of time—usually 20 to 30 days—that the issuer of the credit card allows you to send in your payment before you're charged with interest. Many cards allow such a grace period, but not all. As I've already mentioned, in exchange for certain other privileges such as lower interest rates, some card issuers have eliminated the grace period. Almost invariably, the elimination of the grace period works to the advantage of the lender and the disadvantage of you, the consumer. So you should always be certain that the card you choose provides for a grace period.

Intelligent use of a grace period on a card can be a highly useful tool in the hands of a Power Borrower. This postponement of interest charges in effect gives you a "float," or the free use of the card issuer's money. The float time can be a month or even longer, depending on when you made your purchase and when the grace period ends. Also, the float tends to be longer on charges you make while traveling abroad.

But you have to be careful in making use of the credit card grace period. If you're inattentive, you could allow too much time to elapse, and you might end up paying interest.

One man I know always meant well in trying to make use

of his grace periods. But periodically, he would be distracted by other concerns, and the grace period would pass before he was aware of it. As a result, he ended up paying interest five or six months out of each year—which was certainly not a characteristic of a good borrower.

Some cardholders also fail to leave enough time for their payment to arrive by the due date. If the payment doesn't get to the card company by the due date, you'll be liable for the regular interest charge—even though you may have mailed your bill before that date. To avoid interest, your payment has to *arrive* in the offices of the issuer by the due date. Keep this point in mind if you hold a card with a bill-payment location out of state.

Question 7: Are there automated teller machine outlets for the card? Almost always, this service is presented as an advantage for the consumer—a claim that may or may not be true.

The number of such automated teller machine (ATM) outlets can vary dramatically. Some MasterCards or Visa cards issued by banks, such as Chase Manhattan Bank or Manufacturers Hanover Trust, may offer ten thousand or more ATM outlets around the country. On the other hand, other issuers, such as Bank of America and First National Bank of Boston, have in the past offered no such outlets— though they may offer other emergency cash arrangements with out-of-town banks.

But are these ATM outlets really an advantage? Certainly, it's comforting to know that if you're in a city far from home and you run out of cash, you can get money to tide you over from an ATM or from a bank teller through an emergency cash benefit. On the other hand, the person who regularly makes use of such cash advance services will find him- or herself paying high rates of interest.

My advice: Try to get a card with liberal ATM and emergency cash arrangements—but don't use them unless you really find yourself in an emergency.

Question 8: What free or low-price services and other "special enhancements" are provided through the card? Part of the attraction of owning a credit card may be the access to free or low-priced services that you might not be able to benefit from otherwise. Some of these perks *may* include the following:

• Free travel life insurance when you charge an airline ticket on some cards. The amount may vary from $100,000 to $650,000 or even more if you pay a fee.

• For a few cards, free registration and insurance in case any of your credit cards are lost or stolen. Many card issuers charge a registration fee for this service, which may vary from about $6 to $25 a year.

• Discounts on long-distance phone calls

• Free collision insurance on car rentals

• Credits for the purchase of certain merchandise

• Credits for restaurant charges

• Guaranteed hotel reservations

• Discounts on limousines

• Guest privileges at health clubs

• Use of private offices while you're in transit

• Checking services

• Sweepstakes prizes

In addition to free benefits such as these, many cards also offer extra privileges that you must pay for. Here are a few:

• Automobile road service—which often ranges from an extra $19 to $40 annually

• Discount shopping services—for about $25 to $30 a year

- Legal advice by telephone—for up to $100 annually for a set number of consultations
- Discount travel arrangements for $30 to $35

There may also be arrangements between a credit card and a frequent-flier program sponsored by an airline. In one of these deals, credit card customers can obtain 1,000 miles by signing up for the program, 1,500 miles for the first purchase they make, and then 1 mile of frequent-flier mileage for each dollar they charge thereafter. Under the frequent-flier programs, the miles that have been accumulated may be exchanged for upgrades in service (e.g., coach to first-class) and for free trips.

One additional comment about the credit card–frequent-flier cards: If you're a Power Borrower, this type of Visa card or MasterCard could make a lot of sense. You and your family could earn a trip free of airline expense and avoid interest charges by putting all of your charges on this card *and* paying bills as they arrive—i.e., not on a revolving-balance basis.

If, on the other hand, you're a Weak Borrower, you could be tempted to buy and charge more purchases just to earn miles for some dream trip in the future. So be sure you know yourself before you get involved in one of these deals! If you can't control your charging habits, don't take on one of these cards. By the way, these combination cards usually have an annual fee of $50, or about $30 more than the plain vanilla MasterCard.

Cards with these benefits are available at various banks and other financial institutions. If you have a good credit rating and an annual income above $10,000, you should qualify for many of them. Just check with the local bank branches in your area for application information.

Finally, it's important to explore whether you can qualify for lower interest rates or other benefits by getting a credit card from your home bank. In some cases, if you link your credit card to your savings and checking accounts, you may find yourself in a favored position for better interest rates and service charges.

Question 9: What steps should I take if I think an incorrect charge has been included on my credit card bill? If an incorrect or questionable charge appears on your bill, you should first notify the issuer of the card and ask for additional information, such as copies of charge slips. It's best to make your inquiry immediately by phone to the customer service 800 number indicated on your statement. Then, confirm the conversation in writing to establish a "paper trail" that you can use later if the matter should end up in the hands of lawyers.

If, after investigating the item, you feel that the card issuer is in the wrong, state law may require you to notify the company in writing within a specified period of time, such as sixty days. The issuer will typically have a given period, such as thirty days, to respond. Usually, the issuer will have to either correct the error or tell you why the charge was correct.

During the time that you and the card issuer are discussing the matter, the issuer can keep the disputed item on your statement. The card company can also charge you interest on the unpaid amount if you decide you want to withhold payment until the disputed matter has been settled.

Later, if it becomes clear that the issuer was wrong, the interest charge and the charge for the item must be removed from your record. On the other hand, if *you* turn out to be wrong, you'll have to pay the amount of the charge plus interest.

What if your argument is not with the credit card company, but with the seller about the quality of the item you purchased?

In this case, you should first notify your bank by phone and then follow that up with a confirmation in writing about the matter. If you then make a good faith effort to settle the dispute with the seller, you may be able to refuse to pay for the item and for any finance charges associated with it. But check your local laws and consumer regulations to be certain of your rights before you take this step.

Question 10: What happens if my credit card is lost or stolen?
    As I've already indicated, most credit cards provide for card registration in case a card is lost or stolen. There may be no registration fee, or it may cost as much as $25 annually for the protection of all your credit cards. The way this service works is rather simple: You just register your credit cards with one company, and then you make one call to them if your cards are lost or stolen. The registration service will then notify the issuers of all your credit cards and insure you against any loss.

    I pay $12 a year for this privilege, and I recommend this form of insurance, even though some financial counselors would advise against it. They typically argue that it's as easy to make a few calls to credit card companies as it is to make one call to a registration service. According to the law, if you make those calls before the cards are used, you are no longer liable for unauthorized use. And even if you don't notify the issuers in time, the maximum liability you face is $50.

    But I look at things a little differently. Many cardholders might get rattled after a mugging and forget the proper notification procedures, or others might not realize they had lost their credit cards for a day or so. Also, most people have more than a couple of cards.

    Clearly, there's a real possibility that if your cards are lost or stolen, they'll be used in an unauthorized way, before the credit card issuer has been notified. In such a case, having to pay even a $50 limit on several lost or stolen cards could be rather burdensome. Five stolen cards, for example, could mean a loss to you of $250. So I prefer to play this part of the credit card game rather cautiously and insure my cards with a registration service.

    Also, I have my registration service telephone number

and account number written down in the appointment calendar I carry in my attaché case. That way, even if my purse has been stolen, I can stop any fraud—fast!

One other theft precaution: Try to carry as few cards as possible with you each day. If you're mugged, that practice will minimize the hassle of waiting for replacement cards. Another tip that is especially useful to thwart theft is to keep your cards separate from your wallet. Often, thieves are primarily interested in cash and will steal only a wallet. So by keeping the cards separate, you will reduce the risk of being inconvenienced by loss of both cards and cash.

Even as I go over these important questions that bear on credit cards, I realize that a true Power Borrower shouldn't have to worry about many of them, simply because he or she won't use a credit card in many of the ways we've discussed.

The Power Borrower, for example, most likely:

Won't rely on ATM outlets for cash advances.

Won't become a "revolver" and thus have to worry about high interest rates on credit card loan balances.

Won't hold so many credit cards that he has to worry about an accumulation of annual fees.

Won't inadvertently or intentionally violate grace periods and thereby incur interest or penalty charges.

Will only have the plastic money that matches his or her life-style of sound money management.

At the most, a family should limit their card holdings to an arrangement like this: an American Express *or* Diners Club card; a MasterCard *or* Visa card; a gas company card; a bank-issued ATM access card; and perhaps one or two retail store cards for establishments that the family frequents.

In most cases, however, with a little forethought, this number of cards can probably be cut in half. Despite all the foresight that can be mustered, we all make mistakes at times, and it's all too easy to slip with a credit card. So even for Power Borrowers, the best rule of thumb with plastic money is the less you have the better.

CHAPTER 6

The Float Factor

"Float," in financial jargon, has nothing to do with buoyancy on water! Rather, float is the interest-free use of another's money for a certain period of time. In effect, it's a free loan.

As we'll see, both the lending institution *and* the consumer can make use of float. So it's up to you as a Power Borrower to make sure that *you* are the one who seizes the opportunity and takes advantage of this phenomenon.

Specifically, the term float refers to the time delay between (1) a purchase or payment by means of a credit card or a check, and (2) the final disposition of that payment or check. During the float period, the check or credit card charge literally drifts about in the financial system—and either the consumer or the financial institution is in a position to turn the float to a dollars-and-cents advantage.

THE BASICS OF FLOAT

As you'll recall from one of our previous discussions, there's an important float period with credit card purchases. When you make a purchase with a credit card, you don't have to pay immediately for what you buy. Instead, you in effect get a free loan, often for three weeks or more, until your credit card bill arrives.

A personal illustration: On examination of a recent American Express bill I received, I noticed that charges I had made on April 10 appeared on the statement dated May 25—a delay that gave me more than six weeks of free float.

Even *after* the bill arrives, most cards will provide you a designated grace period of twenty to thirty days during which you can pay without incurring interest or penalties. Or, with the so-called charge cards like American Express, you may be able to wait forty-five days or even longer before you pay— though when you do pay on such a card, you have to pay your bill in full.

Checking accounts provide us with further illustrations of float. Assume that someone gives you an out-of-town check, and you deposit it in your checking account. It always takes a few days—and sometimes a week or more—for such a check to "clear" so that the money becomes available for your use. The delay between the deposit of the check and the availability of the money is the float.

In this case, the float typically works to the advantage of the bank, not the consumer. The bank will have the use of the check writer's money for a time without having to pay any interest for the privilege.

To grasp how this works, it's important to understand first of all that the check-clearing system is divided into two parts.

Part 1. The first stage is very fast, taking at the most about two days to complete, and involves the transport of the check from the bank where it was deposited to the bank on which the check was written. Through the use of sophisticated electronic devices, overnight couriers and the like, the depositing bank really operates as though it's trying to break records to get that check back to the home bank (the payer bank).

Why such a hurry? The depositing bank can then begin to use the funds that have been deposited *as soon as possible*.

Part 2. The second half of the check-clearing process, which is much slower, involves the determination by the bank of when depositors can use the funds from the checks they have deposited.

In one study by *The Wall Street Journal*, eleven banks surveyed responded that their total check-clearance time might vary from three business days to fifteen business days. As if that weren't bad enough, in some situations the entire process has been known to take as many as twenty-two days for an out-of-town check!

Why such a long time for a check to clear completely? One reason for the extra time in the second phase of the process is that questionable or bad checks must be laboriously checked by hand, rather than whisked back to the depositing bank through a high-speed electronic system. As a result, a check that has been written on an account without sufficient funds takes much longer to be returned to the depositing bank than to take that initial trip from the depositing back to the paying bank.

Banking representatives say the extra time is necessary to enable them to avoid losing money through fraud or negligence by those who write checks. They argue that since a great deal of money is potentially involved, they must pay particularly close attention to this part of the check-clearing process. Even though only about 1 percent of checks are returned for insufficient funds each year, those bad checks total $47 billion. And that represents quite a potential loss for the nation's banking system.

But consumer advocates contend that an even more important reason for the delay is that banks want to keep a hold on depositors' funds for as long as possible. In this way, they can use the float from the checks as interest-free loans.

Incredible amounts of money are involved in this check

float issue. Every day, approximately 100 million checks pass through the nation's banking system, and the float from those checks runs into the billions of dollars. In New York State alone, the float time *each week* involves tens of millions of dollars. Banks that can make use of this interest-free float by investing the unreleased funds at the going interest rates can greatly increase their revenues. On the other hand, consumers and businesses can also profit if they gain faster access to their deposited money by cutting down on their float time.

This is not to say that all banks have a "heads we win, tails you lose" policy. Some have an additional feature to their checking accounts that treats your deposits of checks as cash, up to a specific dollar amount—which depends on the level of savings you have with them. In other words, you get instant access to your deposits up to the specified dollar amount. If you're considering a new bank for your checking account, it would be wise to investigate to see what their check-clearing policy is.

Finally, help with this issue may be on the way from the government. Some recent federal legislation has been passed to reduce float time and give consumers faster access to their money—though at this writing, banks and other financial institutions are trying to limit the impact of the new rules.

WHAT'S THE LAW ON THE FLOAT FACTOR?

The federal Expedited Funds Availability Act, which was written to go into effect in two stages in 1988 and 1990, requires a reduction in the time for clearance of deposited funds.

Specifically, on September 1, 1988, the law has provided that the following had to occur:

1. Financial institutions such as banks, savings and loans and credit unions can hold out-of-town checks for as long as seven days after the day of deposit.

2. Checks written on financial institutions in the same metropolitan area or within the same Federal Reserve region have to be cleared within three business days.

3. Government checks, cashier's checks, and certified checks must be available for withdrawal by the depositor on the next business day.

These times will be limited still further in 1990. The maximum clearance time will be two business days for local checks, and five business days for out-of-town checks. The one-day rule for government, cashier's, and certified checks stays the same.

In addition to these provisions, the law gives banks eight days to make funds available in "new" accounts, which are currently defined as accounts that have been in existence for thirty days. These new accounts are traditionally regarded as being more likely to involve fraud than older, more established accounts.

Also, banks get an extra four days to clear deposits in three categories: those involving over $5,000, those in accounts with a history of repeated check-bouncing, and those involving suspicious checks.

As these rules have gone into effect, bankers continue to worry that a situation like the following might occur:

A customer of a Los Angeles bank—who also happens to be a bad-check artist—may deposit a $10,000 cashier's check drawn on a Miami bank. But because of the three-hour time difference, it's impossible for the Los Angeles bank to get in touch that day with the Miami bank, which has already closed. The next morning, the customer-crook in Los Angeles withdraws his funds before any response has come from the

Miami bank. As a result, the Los Angeles bank loses the $10,000—unless it can catch up with the check forger.

Consumer advocates respond that such fraud is relatively rare, and the onus of risk associated with check float should rest on the banks, not on the consumer. If banks hastened the check-verification process, then the banks would be protected and the consumer could benefit from earlier use of the funds.

As these arguments go back and forth, there remains some likelihood that the law on the float factor may change from time to time. But one thing that probably won't change is the existence of check float in some form. So it behooves you, as a Power Borrower, to understand how you can make use of the float on your checks to your own advantage.

HOW YOU CAN TURN FLOAT
TO YOUR ADVANTAGE

You don't have to be a financial wizard to turn check float to your advantage. First, study the details of how your local banks operate with their customer accounts. Then, you'll be in a position to map out the best strategy for your own personal dealings with banks and other financial institutions—and to get the benefit of float rather than giving it to your bank by default. Let me give you a couple of illustrations of how this can work.

One alert consumer, Herb, took advantage of the float on his deposits in this way: He received a substantial check that was drawn on an out-of-state bank. But he knew from experience that it would take more than a week for that check to clear and for the funds to become available in his checking account. So instead of depositing the check in his checking account, he decided to deposit it in his highest-interest *savings* account. This was a money market fund that at the time was paying nearly 1 percent more than his day-to-day savings account.

As you may already know, many savings accounts begin to credit you with interest *immediately* on a deposited check, even if that check hasn't yet cleared. The money doesn't become available for withdrawal until the check clears, but this hold on the funds—this float factor—doesn't affect the accrual of interest.

So Herb's bank began to credit him with interest on the deposited check, even though the funds weren't available for withdrawal. Finally, more than a week later, the check cleared and funds became available for withdrawal. But in the meantime, Herb earned interest on his money. Then, when the check finally did become available, he shifted some of the money over to his checking account, where he could use it for personal expenses.

Over the course of a year, Herb managed on a regular basis to keep thousands of dollars in uncleared checks in his savings account. As a result, he earned several hundred dollars in interest that would have been unavailable to him if he had simply waited out the float period on the checks deposited in a regular checking account.

To use a strategy such as the one adopted by Herb, you'll need to check with your bank to be certain that it pays interest on checks that haven't yet cleared. If you find that your bank doesn't pay interest until the underlying funds become available—and if this approach to float could earn you a significant amount of money—you may want to shop around a find a bank that *does* pay interest immediately.

Of course, there are many other ways that you, as a consumer, can be able to take advantage of float. To explore the possibilities, let me urge you again to take a short period of time, say one evening, to go over your bank statements and list a few ideas on a sheet of paper. Then, you might make a couple of calls to local banks the following day. This was the approach followed by Jan, a self-employed investment consultant—and she managed to make even more money on the float than Herb.

Jan kept a portion of her business funds in an interest-bearing checking account in a brokerage house—an account that required the use of checks from an out-of-town bank. Typically, Jan paid herself a salary out of this account, which usually contained more money than any of her other checking accounts. She kept most of her liquid cash in this account for a couple of reasons:

First, she wanted to take advantage of the relatively high interest paid on money in the account. Like many savings accounts, this interest-bearing brokerage checking account began to pay interest immediately on checks that were deposited, regardless of when the checks cleared. So, like Herb in our previous example, Jan was able to reduce the impact of the float factor on checks she received as payment for her services.

Also, she preferred to be able to cash in her stocks, bonds, or other investments and have the money transferred immediately to the brokerage checking account. That was a quicker and more convenient procedure than having the money sent over to a checking account in some outside institution.

But there was a problem with this approach. You'll recall that Jan usually paid her salary out of the brokerage checking account. But when she deposited a check from her brokerage account into her personal bank checking account, she often had to wait a week or more for the checks to clear. The float factor was working against her in this situation, and that meant she was losing the use of her money.

So Jan sat down with her brokerage and personal banking files and began to make some interesting discoveries. What first caught her eye were her dealings with her local bank, where she had personal savings and checking accounts, and also some lines of credit. She made regular use of her bank's check overdraft privileges and also of an unsecured line of credit, usually to keep her cash flow steady in her business.

But even though the loan privileges kept her business on

an even keel, Jan was paying out more in interest than she wanted. So she found herself wondering, "Is there some way I can eliminate my problems with the float on the brokerage checks I write?" Also, she asked, "Can I reduce my loan interest expenses?"

In fact, her answer to both questions was yes. Furthermore, by employing a rather shrewd strategy, she managed to use her unavailable funds to pay off her loans, get maximum interest income, and turn the float factor to her advantage.

A key part of this financial strategy involved moving money back and forth among several of her accounts. Here are the key elements in her approach:

1. She would first write herself a salary check from her interest-bearing brokerage account, which required the use of those checks from an out-of-town bank.

2. Then, she would endorse the out-of-town check she had just written over to her bank to pay off one of her personal loan accounts.

3. Jan's bank credited her loan payments immediately, and that reduced the interest she was paying out.

4. At the same time, the funds on which she wrote the checks—the money that was on deposit in her interest-bearing brokerage checking account— brought in extra interest to her until the checks cleared.

5. Finally, Jan continued to deposit all checks given to her in payment for her services into her brokerage checking account. And the account continued to pay her interest immediately on those deposits, even though the checks hadn't yet cleared.

As a result, Jan eliminated many of the problems she had been experiencing with float. She increased her cash flow by increasing the interest that was coming in to her, while reducing the interest she was paying out.

Clearly, float can be a very complicated factor. But with some intelligent planning and forethought, it's possible for any consumer to eliminate days, weeks, or months of lost income from inactive, inert deposits that can't be withdrawn because the checks haven't cleared.

As we've seen, there are a number of possibilities that enable the Power Borrower to make profitable use of float:

- You can reduce or eliminate interest on your loans by paying them off with uncleared checks.

- You can earn interest on uncleared checks you've *received* by depositing them in an interest-bearing account.

- You can earn interest during the float period on uncleared checks you've *written* if the funds underlying the ʻchecks remain in an interest-bearing checking account. In this one instance, the float works to the consumer's advantage. Many banks and brokerage firms offer this service.

As you study the rules and practices of your own banking institutions, you'll undoubtedly discover other ways that you can save or earn money by turning the float factor to your advantage. In short, there's every reason why float should become a financial benefit rather than a bane in the hands of the Power Borrower.

CHAPTER 7

Cars on Credit

Buying and selling cars is big business in our society—both for the auto industry and for the nation's major banks. Auto loans themselves have become a billion-dollar service that these two industries provide.

In one recent year, car loans through banks topped $93 billion, and car loans through the three largest carmakers totaled $83 billion. Another $41 billion in loans was written by credit unions and savings and loans. The average outstanding car loan, which requires consumers to make substantial interest payments to the lenders, is about $5,000.

Obviously, large corporations are in a position to make a great deal of money by collecting interest when cars are bought through borrowing. At the same time, the individual consumer, depending on his savvy in the marketplace, can either win big or lose big in purchasing a car on credit.

In this chapter, I want to help you begin your journey through the sometimes exotic and arcane landscape of the car loan business by providing a brief but practical guide to some of the major car loan concepts.

THE POWER BORROWER'S GUIDE
TO BUYING A CAR ON CREDIT

The various car loans that banks, carmakers, and other corporations and financial institutions offer consumers are in a state of constant flux. There is tremendous competition to capture the car loan market. As a result, the potential lenders are always changing and fine-tuning their marketing strategies in an effort to titillate the imaginations of prospective buyers.

Because of the mercurial nature of the auto loan business, it's impossible to provide you with a list of possibilities that are written in stone and valid for future years—or even for the next few months! But what I can do is to give you some idea of the breadth and depth of the car loan potpourri. Then, you'll be in a better position to approach the possibilities as a knowledgeable, powerful borrower.

The traditional bank car loan. Actually, car loans from banks are not often traditional. To meet the challenge of attractive loans from carmakers, banks have been learning to respond with new marketing concepts—and in many cases, that can mean a savings to the consumer.

For example, bankers have noticed that nonbank loans often run for relatively short terms and may be limited to only a particular group of cars. So banks have been offering longer-term loans that allow the buyer to pay back the borrowed funds over a period of sixty months or so. One bank in California has even offered to finance a car loan over a seventy-two month period!

Of course, the consumer may end up paying more in total interest this way than if he or she chooses the shorter-term approach. But the monthly payments for a long-term loan tend to be lower, and that puts less of a cash-flow crunch on the buyer.

In addition to lengthening the terms of car loans, banks have moved to emulate practices of carmakers by instituting variable-rate loans and sometimes even loans without down payments. In addition, banks emphasize that when consumers take out their loans, they enter into a relationship with a "full service" lender. In other words, they can offer mortgages, checking and savings arrangements, and a variety of other financial services not available through carmakers.

Finally, remember that there may be a variation in bank rates for car loans. Many times, you'll find that your own bank will offer you the best interest arrangement because of the fact that you're an established customer.

I did a little loan shopping among the banks in my neighborhood, and I discovered at that time that the interest rate on a two- to five-year car loan varied from 10 to 11 percent for one of the bank's customers. For noncustomers, the rate was considerably higher—12 to 13 percent.

But once again, let me caution you about these rates: They go up and down on a regular basis, and so you should never rely entirely on any figures you read, no matter how current they may seem. It will be up to you to shop around, identify the latest interest rates and then make your own comparisons and decisions.

The hot new carmaker loans. Some of the best auto loan deals may come from the carmakers themselves. But if you get a whiff of what seems to be an incredible loan, don't scoop it up without first doing some checking and testing. There are a variety of possible pitfalls and hidden traps that lurk in these seemingly attractive arrangements. Here are just a few of the considerations, both pro and con, that you should keep in mind if you're considering a carmaker's loan:

• Periodically, carmakers may offer *extremely* low interest rates on car loans. In recent years, for example, American Motors has offered *zero* percent financing, and General Motors has provided 2.9-percent interest rates.

But there's a catch: To get these rates, you usually have to buy the particular model or models that the carmaker is offering for the low-rate loans. Furthermore, you can expect *only* the features that are included with those models, and no other "extras." If a two-door model with air-conditioning isn't specified, you can't get a two-door with air-conditioning—unless you agree to pay a higher interest rate.

Usually, the models that the carmakers offer at these low rates aren't the most popular models. Instead, they tend to be cars that aren't moving too well, and the attractive financing is an incentive to the consumer to get those cars out of the carmaker's and dealer's inventories.

• Sometimes, the car dealer will offer a *rebate* as an alternative to the low-interest loan package. For example, when you go in to buy a $12,000 car, you may be given a chance to choose between a $1,500 rebate or a 2.9-percent loan over thirty-six months. In such a case, should you go for the rebate or the low-rate loan?

Some experts believe that the rebate is almost always the better deal. Here are some sample calculations that show *possible* advantages for a rebate plus bank loan:

If you choose the carmaker's loan package in the above example, your monthly payments would be $348.48. But if you pick the rebate option, you would get the car for $10,500 (the original price of $12,000 minus the rebate of $1,500). Then, suppose you are able to get a bank loan at an annual percentage rate of 9.9 percent. In that case, your monthly payments on the loan would be $338.43. This would represent a monthly savings of $10.05 with the rebate plus bank loan—and a total savings of $361.80 over the life of the loan.

Also, the lower purchase price will mean you'll pay a

lower sales tax if such a tax applies in the area where you're buying the car.

There are other possible benefits with the rebate-plus-bank-loan deal. We've already seen that carmaker loans come with restrictions on the car model and accessories, so a rebate and bank loan would give you more flexibility in choosing exactly the type of car you want. Also, you may end up with a shorter-term loan with higher monthly payments through the carmaker than through the bank.

Obviously, the figures we've used in this example are hypothetical, and so they can only be used to suggest certain courses of action. In the last analysis, it's essential for you to do some research and find the *real* figures that will provide a basis for comparison.

It may be, for example, that the bank loans offered to you will carry such high interest that it won't make sense to pair a bank loan with a rebate. On the other hand, you'll never know what's best for you until you determine the precise figures and interest rates that are available, and then figure out on paper the most attractive deal.

The new graduate loans. Lenders are especially interested in getting the business of young people who are ready to buy their first car. So carmakers, banks and other institutions are offering special deals to recent college graduates.

The terms of the loans include such benefits as those recently offered by the General Motors Acceptance Corporation: Young borrowers were allowed to make a relatively low down payment. Also, they had the option (1) to defer monthly payments for the first three months or (2) to receive a rebate of $250.

The seasonal payment loan. Some lenders arrange car loan payments to conform to the ebb and flow of a consumer's income. For example, if you're a schoolteacher, you will probably be able to find a lender (perhaps your credit union) that will allow you to skip your payments in the summer. Or if you have another seasonal business, such as selling Christmas trees, farming, or fishing, you will probably be able to work out a deal so that you pay only during those months when you're receiving income.

The variable-rate car loan. With this approach, interest rates move up and down during the life of the loan in accordance with the movement of some base interest rate, such as the prime rate.

As with variable-rate credit card interest, many consumers are wary of this concept because they are afraid of getting stuck with very high interest rates if the economy should move in that direction. On the other hand, during some periods in the last few years, variable-rate instruments have had much more attractive interest rates than fixed instruments.

In general, the variable-rate approach seems best for those who are more risk-oriented and not particularly inclined to worry too much about their finances.

The balloon payment car loan. This type of car financing "looks like a lease, but acts like a loan," as one expert has said (*The New York Times*, August 16, 1986). In general, like leases, these balloon loans are set up so that the buyer can get a new car with a minimal down payment and a relatively low monthly payment, in comparison with standard car loans.

An executive from the Ford Motor Credit Company offers this illustration of how such a loan might work:

Assume that you buy a car for $12,000 with a forty-eight-month loan agreement. The lender first determines that the car will be worth $4,000 at the end of the loan period. Also, he requires a down payment of 15 to 20 percent of the purchase price.

According to the contract, the buyer pays about $200 monthly, rather than the $250 he would have to pay for a regular bank loan. Then, when the final, forty-eighth month rolls around, the buyer is presented with several choices:

• He or she can just hand the car over to the dealer for a $250 disposal fee, and that ends the contract.

• He can keep making payments for an additional nineteen to twenty months until the obligation has been completely paid off—and then he will own the car outright. In this case, the total payment time would be about sixty-eight months instead of the originally agreed-upon forty-eight months.

• He can pay off the remainder of the loan in one relatively large lump sum (a "balloon" payment), and become the owner at the end of the forty-eight-month period.

• If the value of the car on the open market is greater than the amount of the final payment of the loan, the buyer can sell the car, pay off the rest of the loan, and pocket the difference.

The balloon-loan concept becomes more attractive when interest rates are relatively high because with the balloon setup, the buyer enjoys much lower payments during the first part of the loan payment period. Lenders who offer this option say that the balloon loan is especially designed to appeal to younger people who want a new car but can't meet the requirements for regular loans.

In addition to the above car-purchase possibilities, there are a number of others that you may want to consider. For example, if you have a home equity loan, you may want to draw upon that to pay for a car—especially if the interest rate is lower than what you can get for a regular car loan.

And remember: The interest you pay on a home equity loan should be fully deductible on your income tax, so long as you meet the requirements outlined in Chapter 10 on the tax consequences of borrowing. In brief, you'll see that the interest on home equity loans is fully deductible. But when the loan exceeds an amount equal to the purchase price of the home, added to any costs of improving the property, the loan funds must be used for medical or educational purposes. Otherwise, the interest on these loan funds is not deductible.

In contrast to interest on a home equity loan, any interest you pay on the other types of car loans I've been describing in this chapter has only limited deductibility through 1990. After 1990, the interest is not deductible at all.

But even with possible low rates and tax breaks, it may not be wise to rely on a home equity loan if the only purchase you plan to make is a car. For one thing, there are usually significant up-front costs on any home loan, including attorney's and appraiser's fees. These expenses may totally eliminate the advantage from lower interest rates or tax deductions.

Another possible source for an attractive car loan is a credit union. If you belong to one of these organizations and have a savings account with it, you might try getting a secured loan for a car with your savings account serving as collateral. Credit unions often have the best deals with this type of loan, and the money that you've put up as collateral will continue to earn interest at the relatively high credit-union rates.

How about just paying for your car in cash? Certainly, the Power Borrower who has plenty of extra cash may want to consider this option. But again, it's important to figure out all the financial details before you take such a significant step. And I use the word "significant" because after all, practically any car you buy—and especially any new car—is going to cost thousands of dollars. If you put such a large lump sum into one item all at once, you should be certain that the dollars-and-cents considerations, including the saving of interest payments, really make sense.

Certainly, buying a car outright for cash would save you a great deal in interest. But you'll have to divert that large payment from other investments or savings accounts. In addition, you won't necessarily get a better price for the car by giving a dealer all his money up front. Some dealers make extra money by selling buyers a financing-insurance package, consisting of insurance for their loan, for accidents and for health. In negotiating for a good price for cash up front, your dealer may resist giving you a good deal because he knows he's going to lose money on that financing-insurance arrangement.

BEWARE OF THE FINE PRINT!

As car loans get more complex and exotic, unwary consumers can lose plenty of money if they're not careful to read the fine print. Indeed, an ability to focus intelligently and alertly on the fine print is one of the main characteristics of the Power Borrower.

A case in point involved one Chevrolet dealership in New York that told consumers it was offering a loan for 12-percent interest. At the time, a 12-percent car loan was an attractive arrangement.

But one consumer noticed that the retail installment contract for the car stated in print that the interest rate was *21 percent*, not 12 percent!

When questioned by the prospective buyer, the salesman said, "Don't worry about it—it's twelve percent." With this assurance, this consumer, as well as many others over a period of weeks, went ahead and signed the agreement.

But in fact, there was something to worry about. This consumer discovered three months later, after he had made two payments on the car, that he was in fact paying 21-percent interest. So the consumer complained to state authorities, and the New York State Attorney General's Office got involved.

In the ensuing investigation, it turned out that the bank that was financing the loans had a deal worked out with the car dealership along these lines:

The arrangement allowed the dealership to pocket the difference between (1) a 12.5-percent guaranteed rate, and (2) a higher rate that the dealer could negotiate with its customers, ranging up to a maximum of 21 percent. After a loan agreement with a customer had been set up, the customer would then make monthly payments for the car loan to the bank. And the bank would send the difference between the 12.5 percent and the higher rate—in our consumer's case, 21 percent—back to the car dealer.

The final result? An agreement was reached whereby more than 250 people who got involved in this car loan arrangement received refunds. Also, the car dealer agreed to refinance the loans for the consumers who had been misled. But neither the car dealer nor the bank was charged with or admitted any wrongdoing.

In general, car loan contracts can be the most difficult to understand, and the terms of complex agreements can work to the detriment of consumers. The lessons from this particular case and others like it can be summed up this way:

- Always read *every word* in your car loan agreement. Don't sign until you understand everything in the contract.

- If possible, have your attorney "vet," or check, the contract. His fee should only run about $100 to $200 unless he gets involved in other matters, such as conducting the negotiations. Believe me, this money will be well spent!

- Don't believe any salesman who says, "The deal we're giving you is what I'm *telling* you about now, *not* what's written in this contract."

In fact, the "deal" is *only* what's covered in writing! The interest rate you must pay and the other terms of the loan agreement are stated right there in black and white, and you and the lender will be bound by those terms and no others.

The Power Borrower must be conscientious in reading and perceptive in understanding every loan agreement he or she signs—and that includes car loans or any other borrowing arrangement. Otherwise, some devastating contractual clause or potentially costly provision may slip through and weaken the borrower's financial position considerably.

ARE YOU SURE
YOU SHOULD BUY THAT NEW CAR?

In some ways, it would have been appropriate to ask this question at the beginning of this discussion of car loans rather than at the end. But I prefer for this issue to remain fresh in your mind as we leave this topic because I think it's absolutely fundamental to your personal finances and to your position as a potential Power Borrower.

Remember: Most people don't *have* to buy a new car. Of course, in some cases, the old one may be falling apart, and a new one is an absolute necessity. But most of the time, all of us can get along on the old one for a while longer. In many cases, we just want a new one because we feel we need a "new toy," or because we want to improve our image, or because the new car somehow makes us feel more successful.

I bring up these points merely to remind you that taking out a car loan may not be a necessity, and may even be unwise for you. If you feel, after evaluating your finances, that such borrowing would be a hardship, you should wait until you can really afford the purchase. After all, taking on a car loan these days is much more of a burden than it was a few years ago, when the interest payments were fully deductible. And if, on top of that tax disadvantage, you feel you would be strapped by such a large obligation, you should postpone the purchase.

Sometimes, those relentless monthly payments and interest rates can wreak havoc on the borrower who has failed to place himself in a relatively strong financial position. One such borrower, Jim, a businessman with a less-than-perfect credit history, came into a bank with a very good story. He admitted he had gone through some serious debt problems in the past. But he vowed that those had all been cleared up. In fact, he was holding down a good job and seemed to have made considerable progress in straightening out his finances.

On checking Jim's credit rating, the banker discovered, as he had expected, that the TRW record showed several difficulties with Jim's credit. On the other hand, most of those were more than a year old. Also, Jim emphasized that he had held a good job for about three years and he needed an attractive new car to travel back and forth to various customers.

"I absolutely have to have a nice-looking car to do my work properly," he said. "I've been doing quite well at work—you can check with my boss about that. But image is important in what I do, and the old rattle trap I drive now works against me. I'm ashamed to suggest to clients that they drive around with me because I simply don't *look* as prosperous and successful as I really am."

The argument sounded plausible; Jim was a convincing salesman. Also, his references held up. So the banker decided to take a chance on the car loan.

For five or six months, Jim made his payments on time. But then, he began to get delinquent. In a couple of subsequent meetings with the banker, he revealed that he was feeling some financial pressure, and he was going steadily deeper into debt with an overdraft account at the same bank.

This particular banker moved to another branch of the bank, but Jim's problem persisted. He finally stopped making any payments at all on the car loan, and the bank began collection procedures against him. Because the bank officer who had originally handled the account was the last contact the bank had on record with Jim, the banker's superiors continued to ask questions and demand information about the situation.

Eventually, Jim responded to the bank's threats and worked out a repayment schedule that was extremely burdensome for him and his family. But there was no alternative. He had borrowed from an extremely weak position, and he paid a high price, both financially and emotionally. When he realized that his old bad habits in handling credit had returned, his self-esteem dropped to an all-time low. His self-confidence also declined, and so did his sales performance.

There's no doubt that Jim needed a car for his work. But before he got involved in this car loan situation, he should have put his own finances and budget in better order. As it was, he placed both himself and the banker who had trusted him into a very difficult position. Furthermore, his credit history once again showed he was a Weak Borrower. So it was going to take quite a few years for him to rub his slate clean.

For most of us, the purchase of the kind of auto we want and need can't be accomplished easily by a single lump-sum payment. As a result, some sort of financing is usually necessary. But my advice would be to follow these steps:

Step 1. First, determine the kind of car you really *need*. Sort out and discard those fantasies about having a certain make or model of car as a status symbol. After all, a car is a consumer item that should be used, not simply displayed.

Step 2. Save up as much money as you can for the specific purchase of buying the car *before* you approach a car dealer, and certainly before you sign any contract. Usually, this means you'll have to start months—and maybe even a year or more—in advance to set aside these funds.

With a sizable car fund in your bank, you'll find you have much more flexibility: You can offer to make a large down payment; or you can draw on those funds to make many of your monthly payments; or if you contribute long enough to the fund as you're shopping around, you may even find you have enough money to buy the car outright.

Step 3. Spend some time shopping around and negotiating with dealers. Don't forget, too, to check various banks and your credit union if you're a member of one. Explore the various loan options and concepts we've been discussing in the previous pages.

Step 4. Read any loan agreement you sign *very* carefully, and be ready to call on your attorney to help you with anything you don't understand.

Step 5. Be certain that any debt you incur doesn't cause your total installment debt payments, excluding mortgage payments, to exceed 5 percent of your after-tax income. And remember: The Power Borrower should strive to push that debt payment percentage down to 1 percent of after-tax income.

CHAPTER 8

The Student Loan
Stew

News reports these days are packed with warnings about the alarming rise of college tuition and fees—and the pressure is mounting on parents and students to find better ways to come up with the cash to finance an education. Consider this sampling of panic-promoting headlines that have emblazoned the pages of some of our major newspapers and magazines in the last couple of years:

- AS TUITION RISES TWICE AS FAST AS INFLATION, ARGUMENTS GROW MORE HEATED — *The New York Times*, May 12, 1987

- TRACKING TUITION: WHY COLLEGE FEES ARE RISING SO SHARPLY — CULPRITS INCLUDE BIGGER FACULTY, MORE RECRUITING—*The Wall Street Journal*, December 11, 1987

- WHEN FINANCIAL AID IS NOT ENOUGH: FAMILIES ARE HOCKING THEIR HOMES AND PUTTING STUDENTS TO WORK—*Money*, September 1986

- GET SMART ABOUT FUNDING YOUR CHILD'S COLLEGE EDUCATION: START YEARS AHEAD FOR THE BEST SAVINGS—*Business Week*, March 3, 1986

With such words confronting us practically every time we open a newspaper or magazine, it's no wonder that anxiety has been intensifying about where to get the money for college! And the facts tend to back up the upsetting news reports.

Tuition for the nation's private four-year colleges soared upward by an average of 141 percent during the ten years between 1977 and 1987, according to a survey by the College Board, a national admissions organization. That compares with a smaller 87-percent rise in the consumer price index over the same ten-year period. At the time this book went to press, the cost of one year in college in many of the top schools—including tuition, fees, room, and board—had already risen above $17,000.

The reasons for these rises are manifold, and include such factors as the hiring of extra faculty members, increased recruiting efforts, and higher administrative costs. But these explanations aren't really our concern here: What you're probably most interested in are the answers to a couple of key questions:

1. What is my child's education going to cost?
2. How am I going to afford it?

The answer to the first question is fairly straightforward: The basic cost will be determined by what the college charges for tuition, fees, room, and board—plus other necessary expenses like books and transportation.

The answer to the second question usually depends on how well you and your youngster make use of the four major sources for college funding.

- Contributions from parents' savings or current income
- Scholarships
- Earnings and savings of the student
- Educational loans

Of course scholarships are the best way of paying for an education because they involve an outright grant of money for academic excellence, athletic accomplishment, special financial need, or some other purpose. But scholarship money is quite limited, and most likely, no scholarship your child qualifies for will cover all expenses.

An industrious student can also earn money through a part-time job and that will help defray some of the costs. But again, it's highly unlikely that most youngsters will be able to "work their way through college," given the extremely high cost of an education these days.

Perhaps the best solution of all is to pay for your child's education entirely out of your current income. If you can do so without putting too much of a squeeze on your life-style, that's wonderful. But this approach involves a very big "if." Unfortunately, few families can generate sufficient income to achieve this objective, especially if they have to put more than one child through college.

A more reasonable solution, within the reach of many more families, is to begin years ahead to save money to cover the cost of a child's education. And certainly, I'm the first to recommend that Power Borrowers plan in advance to accumulate money for onerous expenses like college costs. So if you have a few years left before your first child enters college, I'd strongly advise you to begin a systematic savings program designed to help you put money aside for educational purposes. This can be done in several ways:

- A savings account set up in the parent's name

- A savings account set up in your child's name—though you must remember that income above $1,000 earned annually on the account of a child under fourteen years of age will be taxed at the parents' income tax rate

- College tuition prepayment plans

• One of a variety of other investment programs
that your stockbroker or personal financial planner
can describe to you.

The Power Borrower should by all means explore and try
to make use of one or more of these methods of funding a
child's education. If they can be pursued successfully, they
will put him or her at a major advantage in paying educational
expenses.

But let's be realistic. Most people may be able to piece
together part of the costs of college from prior savings, current
income, a child's earnings and perhaps a scholarship. But
usually, that won't be enough.

Suppose, for instance, that your child gets into an
expensive college this year—at a cost of about $15,000 annu-
ally, once you add in transportation expenses and other
incidentals. That's what happened to Ann and Jeff, whose son
Mark was just admitted to a top-level school.

They knew their youngster was bright and qualified, but
to some extent, Ann and Jeff were caught by surprise. A
top-flight college was always a possibility, but now that Mark
had a place in the next freshman class, they wondered, "How
on earth are we going to pay for this?"

Their family income was well above average—about
$45,000 a year. But after mortgage payments, basic living
expenses, and the costs of caring for Mark and their other
youngster, a daughter Sara who was three years younger than
her brother, they found that very little was left over each
month to pay for an expensive college education. Not only
that, as they looked forward three years hence, when Sara
would be ready for college, they realized that they would
probably be facing *another* set of college costs that would be
equally unaffordable.

In going over their budget and their sources of payment
for Mark's college costs, Jeff and Ann came up with these
possibilities:

• They could divert $4,000 from current income each year if they cut far back on their other expenses, such as family entertainment and vacations.

• They could come up with another $3,000 that they expected that Mark could earn from a summer job he had lined up.

• They felt comfortable dipping into a small family savings account for another $2,000.

• Finally, Mark had been awarded a total of $3,000 in various scholarship stipends.

Also, they learned that they might be able to take out a small home equity loan. But they preferred not to go that route because they had just bought their home and had built up relatively little equity in it as yet. Typically, the amount you can borrow with one of these loans is 80–90 percent of the market value of the home, minus the principal outstanding on the mortgage.

The total this family had at their disposal for Mark's education amounted to $12,000. That still left another $3,000 if they hoped to cover the other costs for the first year. Where could they turn? One answer: an education loan.

Ann and Jeff began an exploration of the complex, and sometimes arcane world of the college loan, a world populated by such terms, initials, and acronyms as "Sallie Mae," "Perkins Loans," "GSL," "SLS," and "PLUS." Eventually, they managed to get loans from both Mark's college and from a commercial bank to cover the remaining $3,000 necessary for the first year's college costs.

To understand how this family, as well as many other parents and children, succeeded in getting sufficient loan funds for college, it's necessary to take an excursion into the cryptic language and specialized concepts of the college loan. With a knowledge of this world, the Power Borrower can then tackle the problem of college costs from a position of maximum strength.

IT ALL BEGINS WITH A "DIRECT" APPROACH

The lowest interest rates for educational loans usually can be found in the National Direct Student Loan, also known as the NDSL or the Perkins Loan.

With this type of loan, you must apply directly to your college financial-aid office and establish some financial need. In general, a family must have income of less than $30,000 annually and also meet other financial need tests, which are set by individual colleges and vary according to the policies of the institutions.

Under the current rules, a total of $9,000 in loans is available for an undergraduate over his college years, and a cumulative total of $18,000 is available for graduate students (including any amounts borrowed as an undergrad under this program).

If you qualify for this loan, the repayment schedule is quite attractive. There's no interest charge during the time the student spends in school or for six months after graduation. When the repayment process begins, the interest rate is relatively low on the unpaid balance. (As I write this, the rate is 5 percent a year, as compared with 8 percent for the federally backed Guaranteed Student Loan and 12 percent on federally backed loans taken out by parents.)

For some students and parents, qualifying for this Perkins Loan may be enough to cover college costs. But these loans tend to be harder to get than other types. Also, even if you get a Perkins Loan, it will often take more money to pay all educational expenses.

GETTING TO KNOW SALLIE MAE

If you don't qualify for à Perkins Loan at your school, or if the amount of money available through these loans isn't enough, it will be wise to become aware of Sallie Mae. "Sallie Mae" is the popular name for the Student Loan Marketing Association, a federally chartered corporation that performs several important student loan functions, including:

- The purchase of student loans from commercial financial institutions, like banks
- The sale of securities to raise money to cover student loans
- The extension of money as secured loans to lenders, who in turn make more student loans available

With this federal backing for educational loans, more money has become available at relatively low interest rates to students and their parents. In particular, Sallie Mae has been instrumental in developing two major types of loans: (1) the Guaranteed Student Loans (GSL), and (2) the Parent Loans for Undergraduate Students (PLUS).

The Next Step: Guaranteed Student Loans (GSL)

The federally sponsored Guaranteed Student Loan program is the nation's largest single source of credit for education on the college level or above. Families with incomes below $30,000 a year immediately qualify for one of these loans. Those with higher incomes may also be eligible if they can show sufficient need, such as other heavy financial obligations or other children in college.

How much money can you borrow with this type of loan? For the first two years of college, you can get up to $2,625 a year, and for subsequent years, up to $4,000 annually. The total amount allowed for undergraduate study is $17,250 in loans. Graduate students can receive up to $7,500 annually, with an aggregate amount for graduate study of $54,750, including any undergraduate loans taken out under this program.

There is a maximum 8-percent interest rate on these loans, and interest rates are deferred until six months after the student leaves school. Also, there's a loan fee of 5 percent of the amount borrowed and an insurance fee of up to 3 percent of the amount borrowed. Usually, these fees are deducted from the loan check. The minimum monthly payment is $50, and the term of the loan may run from five to ten years, depending on the amount borrowed.

What if you *still* can't put together enough money to cover costs, even with a GSL and other sources of funds at your disposal? The next line of attack involves loans available to parents of students.

Parent Loans for Undergraduate Students (PLUS)

Parents of financially dependent undergraduate, graduate, and professional students are eligible for a PLUS loan, which is designed to help make up the difference a family needs to finance a child's education.

Unlike some of the other educational loans, you don't have to demonstrate any limit to your income or financial need to borrow under the PLUS program. But there are restrictions on the amount of money you can borrow.

First, the total amount you can borrow in any one year can't be greater than the total cost of the education minus all other financial aid. In other words, the PLUS loan is indeed a "plus" instrument in that it's supposed to be used to *supplement* other financial assistance.

Also, there are dollar borrowing limits: Applicants can only receive up to $4,000 annually per year for each student, or up to $20,000 throughout college for each student. These amounts, by the way, *don't* include amounts borrowed under the GSL program; they are *in addition to* the GSL loans.

The interest rates on these loans are higher than on the Perkins Loans or on loans under the GSL program, and the terms are tougher. Right now, the top rates are 12 percent annually *and* borrowers have to begin to repay the loan while the student is still in school. The rates are determined annually by adding 3.75 percent to the average bond equivalent yield of recently issued 9-day treasury bills.

As for the specifics of repayment, borrowers must begin to make regular payments of principal plus interest two months after the loan is received, with a minimum monthly payment of $50. The length of repayment varies according to the amount borrowed and the annual adjustments to the interest rate.

A *"Plus"* for Students:
Supplemental Loans for Students (SLS)

If you are an undergraduate student and financially independent of your parents — or if you're a graduate or professional student — you may qualify for a Supplemental Loan for Students (SLS).

This SLS loan is similar to the PLUS loan and, in fact, is often lumped in with the PLUS loan by Sallie Mae administrators.

But there's a big difference in the circumstances surrounding the SLS loan, as opposed to the PLUS instrument: With the SLS, the student must be independent, whereas in the other situations we've been discussing, we've assumed that the student was dependent on his or her parents. As we'll see shortly, this distinction can have some important implications for other forms of aid.

But first, a word about the specifics of the SLS: Many of the benefits and requirements are similar to the PLUS loan. For one thing, you can borrow up to $4,000 a year, in addition to any amounts you may have borrowed under the GSL program. Like the PLUS loan, the aggregate amount an undergraduate is allowed to borrow is $20,000.

Also, as with the PLUS loan, there are no income limits that are placed on those who borrow under the SLS program. And the total amount that can be borrowed in any one year can't exceed the cost of the education, minus all other financial aid.

There are other similarities: The annual interest rate may vary, but can't exceed 12 percent per year. Also, the minimum monthly payments are $50, and the length of repayment varies according to the amount borrowed and annual adjustments to the interest rate.

On the other hand, certain of the repayment requirements for the SLS are different from those of the PLUS loan. Independent students who borrow under the program must repay *interest* payments while they're still in school. Repayment of the principal plus interest begins when the student leaves school or drops below full-time attendance.

Dependent or Independent? That is the Question!

If you have a choice, is it best to become an independent student with an SLS loan, or stay dependent on your parents with the PLUS program?

To the degree possible, it's important for the parents and the child to sit down and talk over what's best for everyone concerned in choosing a college. Too often, these decisions may be made on the spur of the moment, or in a vacuum devoid of pertinent facts. Yet most parents really are deeply interested in their child's education, and so it's important for both Mom and Dad and the student to work out a solution together.

For that matter, even parents who tend to be preoccupied with their own affairs are often interested in where their child goes to school, and also in successfully financing the schooling. The child's education is a matter of pride and self-respect for most parents, and the issue of educational expenses may be a way to enhance or improve the parent-child relationship.

Whenever possible, it's probably best from a financial point of view for the student to remain a dependent. I'm reminded of one college student who had assumed it would be best to move out of the house and establish residency in a state where he was thinking about going to school. He had lived in various places independently from his parents, so he was able to establish his lack of dependency on his parents for purposes of the SLS program.

Also, apart from the circumstances under which he had been living, this young man had a special motivation to go for the SLS loan, rather than an instrument that his parents would have to sign. He recalled that years before, his father had taken out a student loan and failed to pay it back. He was afraid that if he put his father's name on a loan application, that would hurt his chances of getting any money.

But even though he succeeded in establishing his independence, this student was turned down when he applied for a loan for an unexpected reason: The school said that because of his income from high-paying part-time and summer jobs— though they amounted to less than $20,000 a year—he had earned enough on his own to pay for his college expenses! His financial obligations as a single person just weren't heavy enough to allow him to qualify!

Had the student foreseen this outcome, he might have planned his life differently. For one thing, he might have been more prudent in saving a large share of his unusually high earnings.

Remember: Even though there are no income limits for an SLS loan, lenders still look at the applicant's financial means. According to the rules, the total amount borrowed in any year can't exceed the cost of the education *minus* all other financial aid. In this case, the amount he made from his jobs was enough to cover the cost of his education and still allow him to meet his daily living expenses. As a result, this young man wasn't entitled to borrow anything under the SLS program.

In most cases, student loan experts confirm the lesson from this example: They say for borrowing purposes, it's usually best for the student seeking a loan not to be independent.

On the other hand, if a student's parents have a moderate income and the student remains dependent on them, the chances are fairly good that the family can qualify for some sort of loan, such as those available under a combination of the GSL and PLUS programs. It tends to be easier and more believable for an entire family to demonstrate that family income is being used and absorbed by family expenses, than it is for an individual student to show that his income is being absorbed only by his own expenses.

There are many other educational loan possibilities, in addition to those that we've been discussing. For example, you can take out a home equity loan or second mortgage and if the loan is used for educational purposes, you can always deduct the interest on your income tax return.

Also, there are a variety of loans available through state agencies and individual college programs. To find out what's available at your college, you should check with the financial aid office there. But whatever avenue of loan funds you try, *always* borrow *only* if you are confident about and committed to an acceptable repayment schedule. If you take out an educational loan without the will or means to repay, you could be borrowing more trouble than money.

PLAN TO REPAY!

Like any other debt, educational loans can impose an unbearable burden on families that are not careful about wise management of their personal budgets.

According to a congressional study released in 1986 by the Joint Economic Committee, increasing numbers of college students are borrowing more money under federal programs. One of the reasons for the mounting debt is that less money has become available in the last decade from grants, which don't have to be repaid. Furthermore, with the soaring student loan debt, which tripled in the ten years from 1976 to 1986, fears have risen that the loan load will undercut the financial stability and strength of the younger generation.

Students in private four-year colleges who took out student loans accumulated an average debt of $8,950 at graduation, the report said. Those in public colleges were nearly as bad off, with average debts of $6,685. Total borrowing under federal programs amounted to $9.8 billion in 1986, as compared with $3.5 billion in 1986 dollars in 1976.

What has been the impact of this huge and growing debt in personal, individual terms?

One in ten students in public colleges and more than a quarter of private-school students owe $10,000 to $15,000 on graduation, and many owe even more. The situation gets still worse for those students who go on to graduate school.

Education experts also fear that the prospect of heavy debts may drive many students away from low-pay public service careers and also encourage them to wait increasingly long periods before they consider beginning a family life.

A potentially even more serious consequence of this burgeoning debt load is an increasing number of loan defaults—a result that could both jeopardize the nation's student loan structure and also seriously damage the future financial position of individual students and their families.

From 1979 to 1987, school loan defaults surged fourfold, to about $1.26 billion a year for a total of nearly $6 billion, according to a study sponsored by the National Governors Association and the National Conference of State Legislators. In fact, the study revealed that 427 colleges and universities had default rates of more than 60 percent among their students. Those sponsoring the study urged the federal government to withdraw guaranteed loan eligibility for sixty-eight colleges and other schools with the worst default records.

As a result of this study and others, the federal government has moved to establish tougher student loan guidelines—which may make hundreds of schools ineligible for federal aid. This pressure on the schools may, in turn, cause school financial-aid officials to be stricter with students and their families who hope to borrow.

Of course, the policy of enforcing tough student loan rules will vary from administration to administration. But with the recent emphasis on fiscal responsibility in government, you can expect those administering loan funds to be more careful about schools and students to whom they lend money.

One of the most disturbing trends for students is the way that government agencies are going after students who are delinquent on their loan payments. The U.S. Department of Education has established a policy that those who haven't paid up or at least reached a repayment agreement on repaying their loans will be billed for collection costs. These costs could amount to as much as 39 percent of the original loan, experts say.

And if the students still refuse to pay what they owe? "We sue!" an Education Department spokesman has declared.

In addition to these measures, the Department of Education will notify credit organizations about defaults. Furthermore, tax refunds of delinquent borrowers can be withheld to pay for the outstanding loan balance.

Clearly, getting in too deep with educational loans can be a serious business. As desirable a thing as an education is, it's not worth the expense to go so far into debt that your personal finances end in a shambles.

SHOULD YOU HIRE A FINANCIAL-AID PLANNER?

Because of the squeeze on educational loans and grants, a new breed of financial-aid expert has arisen in recent years. Some people who have used these planners—who can be found in listings in the Yellow Pages or through referrals—have saved money and increased their financial-aid sources by such means as:

• Gaining access to information about loans, scholarships, and other funds that may not have come to their attention in their own research

• Having an expert representative spend time on educational planning that they themselves couldn't devote to the subject because of other demands and commitments

• Restructuring their personal finances so as to place themselves in a stronger position to qualify for aid

As far as this last point is concerned, some families have followed advice to transfer savings from their child's name to the parents'. As a result of this test, they have qualified for more aid. The reason for this improvement in their aid chances is that schools typically expect a child to use up 35 percent of his personal assets to help pay for college, while parents aren't expected to expend that large a percentage.

Also, some planners have recommended that parents shift as many of their assets as possible into retirement accounts, insurance policies, or annuities. The value of these assets doesn't have to be listed on financial-aid applications, and with lower assets on record, a family is likely to qualify for larger amounts of aid. Assume, for instance, that parents with a $50,000 annual income shift $4,000 in assets to retirement or other funds. According to at least one planner, these parents can expect to reduce by as much as $300 the amount that a college will expect them to contribute to their child's education.

Is there anything wrong with restructuring assets in this way? One official in the U.S. Department of Education has said that it's apparently legal. But he notes there may be a question about the ethics involved.

The main ethical argument that's made against this procedure is that relatively well-to-do families may be able to make themselves appear to be poorer than they really are. As a result, they may be in a position to divert financial-aid funds away from families that are in greater need of the money.

On the other hand, financial planners and other experts contend that the same point could be made about those who know how to save money by getting savvy experts to help them fill out their income tax returns. Those without expert advice may pay more in taxes, but does that make it wrong for others to make use of legal loopholes? Also, proponents of financial-aid planning say, scholarships and other financial aid may go unused because many people simply don't know how to apply for it effectively.

Whatever the merits of these arguments, one thing seems clear: The Power Borrower should avail himself of every scrap of available information to get the best loan deals and other financial aid that is available.

On the other hand, that doesn't necessarily mean that you should go right out and hire a financial-aid planner. These planners can be quite expensive, and they're not regulated by the government. As a result, if you enlist the aid of one of these people without doing a great deal of checking, you may find that you have paid a lot of money for a lot of bad advice. And once the time has passed for applying to various colleges, you and your student may not be in a position to regroup and try again.

In general, if you have the money for one of these planners and you have some *solid* references so that you are sure the person has a good track record, you might try this approach. But with the information in this chapter at your fingertips, it's likely that a good accountant or guidance counselor will be able to do just as much for you.

To sum up, then, as you embark on your search for educational funding, keep these steps in mind:

Step 1: Evaluate your personal income and assets and see how much you can pay toward your child's education.

Step 2: Begin to save right now toward building up a fund to cover at least part of the college costs — even if you're getting started late, every bit helps!

Step 3: Check your child's assets and income and see how much is available there.

Step 4: Pursue opportunities for outright grants and scholarships that don't have to be paid back.

Step 5: Investigate the relatively low-priced National Direct Student Loan, or Perkins Loan.

Step 6: If you still need money, check on a Guaranteed Student Loan (GSL).

Step 7: An important backup borrowing possibility is the Parent Loan for Undergraduate Students (PLUS).

Step 8: If you're an independent student—i.e., not legally dependent on your parents—look into a Supplemental Loan for Students (SLS).

Step 9: Seek outside help for planning your financial-aid package by consulting with free guidance counselors and your accountant. If you have a *good* lead on a professional financial-aid planner, you might also want to explore that possibility—but be sure to look closely before you leap!

Step 10: Establish a repayment plan and schedule—and *do repay!*

CHAPTER 9

Big-time Borrowing: The Home Mortgage Issue

The biggest single investment that many individuals or families make is in their home—and the main way they pay for that investment is through a mortgage.

Simply defined, a mortgage is a pledge of your property as security for the payment of a debt to a bank or other lending institution. Among other features of ownership, you retain the right in the mortgage agreement to occupy the property. But if you fail to pay off your debt to the bank, the bank can "foreclose," or take over the property to cover the money you owe.

Sound simple? It isn't. There are as many varieties of mortgages being offered now as there are fresh vegetables in your local grocery store. And there are even more approaches to mortgage terms by individual bankers—as I discovered in a personal house hunt I conducted in the rolling hills of Connecticut.

SANDY'S HOUSE HUNT

I decided recently that I wanted to buy a house, and Connecticut seemed a reasonable location. The area generally provided easy access to New York City's metropolitan area, where I do much of my work as a marketing consultant.

I wanted a house priced in the $215,000 to $220,000 range, *if* I could get the right kind of mortgage and interest rate. I was willing to make a down payment of 20 percent, or about $40,000 to $45,000. That would leave a mortgage of about $175,000, which I hoped would carry an interest rate of 10.25 percent of so. At the time of my house hunt, by the way, the prime rate was 9 percent.

Also, I wanted a thirty-year mortgage, which I felt would enable me to keep my monthly payments relatively low and help me manage my personal cash flow more easily. I knew I was not a financial risk-taker, so I decided I would have to have a *fixed-rate mortgage*, as opposed to a *variable-rate instrument*. Besides, I expected interest rates to rise substantially within the next two years. That meant a fixed-rate instrument would be best for me, though initially it would be more expensive than the variable-rate type.

Finally, I was willing to pay an *origination fee* to the bank of up to two *points*, or 2 percent of the principal amount I would have to borrow. An origination fee is a professional fee you pay to the bank to cover the booking of the loan. (*Note:* It's not the same as an application fee, which involves a separate payment.) The origination fee is expressed in points: One point is 1 percent of the mortgage you take out. Usually, when you pay one or more points, it makes quite a difference in the rate—say about .25 percent less in interest per point. So, on a $175,000 mortgage, I could reduce my interest rate by .5 percent by paying two points up front.

I calculated that for me, the difference between 10.5 percent and 10 percent in monthly payments would be $65. That's $780 per year, and $23,400 over the lifetime of the mortgage. In short, this 2 percent up front in the form of points—i.e., $3,500—seemed a relatively painless way to reduce my mortgage payments.

My accountant had also advised me that this origination fee involving the payment of points would be tax-deductible in the tax year in which I took out the mortgage. This tax advantage, by the way, applies only to mortgages on a principal residence. If the house being purchased is a second home, the origination fee must be amortized over the life of the loan. For me, such a tax break would be a big plus.

After several weeks of searching, my realtor and I finally found a piece of property that met my needs, at the price I felt I could pay. So I launched my next effort—finding a bank that would give me the kind of mortgage I needed. In addition to my personal requirements, my prospective seller posed one of his own: He was quite eager to sell the home. So he wanted me to show evidence within two to three weeks that I had a mortgage commitment from a bank.

Note: It's necessary to have your real estate offer accepted by a seller before you go out looking for a bank. I had approached a couple of banks, asking, "Can you qualify me for a mortgage *before* I have an acceptance from a seller?"

All the bankers replied that they had to appraise the property before they granted the mortgage. Also, they said, a mortgage agreement always relates to a specific piece of property. As a result, I learned, I'd have to wait until I had an understanding with a seller before I could apply.

With these facts and conditions in mind, I set out to find a bank that would handle my mortgage business. My realtor and attorney, who knew the Connecticut area better that I did, referred me to several local savings and commercial banks, and also to one major New York bank that had a mortgage subsidiary in Connecticut. In some cases, they gave me the name of actual bankers to contact. This sort of personal entree to the banking community can be quite helpful when you're looking for a large loan, such as a mortgage. But as we'll see, these contacts certainly don't assure you'll get a mortgage.

Now here, bank by bank, is an account of my adventures with the vagaries and vicissitudes of the Connecticut mortgage scene.

Bank # 1. This institution, a savings bank, offered only a one-year variable-rate mortgage at 11-percent interest—a mortgage whose rate can fluctuate annually. I knew that this type of loan, which would start out at a higher rate than I wanted to pay, could increase to 15 percent or more, as had happened within the previous eight years. So I scratched this possibility!

Bank # 2. This local commercial bank also offered only variable-rate mortgages, though they were cheaper than those of Bank # 1.

Specifically, this lender had rates of 9.5 percent, and as a starter, that looked pretty attractive. But under the terms of their agreements, the bank could raise the rates as much as 2 percent in any year, up to a ceiling of 5 percent additional interest over the life of the mortgage. In other words, I could be paying 14.5 percent if their rates increased.

Also, this bank would require that I keep on deposit in an interest-bearing account funds ranging in amount from 10 percent to 15 percent of the amount I'd be borrowing. That is, I'd have to keep on deposit an extra $17,000 to $25,000 of my money with this institution.

Bank # 3. This savings bank told me that I couldn't get a fixed-rate mortgage from them either. The reason? I wanted to borrow more than the loan lid of $168,700 established by "Fannie Mae," the Federal National Mortgage Association. This bank followed closely the Fannie Mae guidelines.

But their variable rate was the best I had encountered: 7⅝ percent, plus two "points" as an origination fee. On the other hand, the cap on their interest rate was an extra 6 percent, which meant I could be paying a total of 13⅝ percent on the mortgage if rates rose.

Also, this institution presented an insurmountable problem with approval of a mortgage: Because they did their mortgage business through a major commercial bank in Boston, the turnaround time on an approval would be about six weeks, or far longer than the time required by my seller.

By now, I was getting worried. I had found an acceptable house, but for one reason or another, I couldn't find an acceptable way to finance it. Refusing to give up, however, I moved on to the next possibility.

Bank # 4. The representatives of this bank, a large commercial institution based in New York City, first said they couldn't do anything for me with a fixed-rate mortgage because of the Fannie Mae lid of $168,700. But my attorney came to the rescue at this point. "That's impossible," he said, "because I'm handling a purchase right now that's being financed by that bank for two hundred forty thousand dollars."

So I placed another call to the banker I'd been dealing with and asked him to recheck what he had been telling me. The man assured me he would get back to me within an hour—but I didn't hear from him until three days later. At that time, he reported, "Yes, we can do it, but the fixed rate will be eleven and a quarter percent."

The rate was a little too high, but what bothered me most was the delay in contacting me. This institution apparently couldn't handle a routine telephone inquiry in one business day, even though the banker had said he would call. So I found I lacked confidence in whether the institution could process my mortgage application in a timely manner. In any case, I wasn't impressed.

Bank # 5. This savings bank also offered only a variable-rate arrangement, and their best interest was 8.5 percent, with two points (2 percent of the amount to be borrowed) required as an origination fee.

But the negatives were overwhelming: (1) a required down payment of 25 percent, which was more of my liquid assets than I planned to use; and (2) an estimated approval time of up to four weeks, a delay that would cause my seller to turn elsewhere.

Bank # 6. Finally, I encountered a ray of hope! This sixth savings bank offered me a fixed, thirty-year mortgage, which would only require a 20-percent down payment. And the interest was close to my target of 10.25 percent. This seemed to be what I was looking for.

Also, they had an innovative product that involved a reduced mortgage rate if I made my payments biweekly. Specifically, with a twenty-six-week payment cycle per year, I could save ⅛ of 1 percent on the interest rate. This way, if I wanted, I could pay the mortgage off in twenty-two years instead of thirty, and in the process, I could save over $150,000 over the lifetime of the loan!

Finally, the turnaround time for the mortgage was excellent—a guaranteed ·twelve business days for them to make a formal decision.

Needless to say, I applied to this bank, and I came prepared to the teeth for the meeting with the loan officer. I brought two years of income tax returns—a necessary bit of evidence since I'm self-employed. Also, I had my financial accounts records, which show the amount of financial assets I have in each of my investment vehicles. These included stocks, mutual funds, retirement accounts, and money market funds. Also, I supplied various account numbers for checking and savings accounts, credit cards, and other financial instruments.

The banker did his necessary calculations as I sat there with him, and he gave me verbal approval right on the spot. Of course, for the commitment to be official, the bank had to do a more complete check of my credit history, verify my balances with the banks and other holdings, and conduct an appraisal of the house. Still, I was sure I had found the right bank, and the way had now been cleared for a purchase of the property.

What are the messages or lessons I derive from this experience?

In the first place, it's clearly not easy to find just the right bank for one particular set of needs. I could have compromised at any point in my bank search, such as by deciding to take a variable-rate mortgage instead of a fixed-rate instrument. But in the long run, that would have been an unacceptable course for me to take.

I know myself well enough to understand this: If I had gotten involved with a variable interest rate that could move up with the interest market, I could easily have become distracted or worried about how I was going to meet the payments or relieve the increasing financial pressures.

So despite the temptations to the contrary, I stuck with my basic strategy, including the interest rate and other terms that I knew I could live with. Finally, after considerable shopping and negotiating among six lending institutions, I found the one that met my needs.

With this personal introduction to the mortgage market in mind, let's turn now to some of the other key elements that characterize big-time mortgage borrowing.

THE BASICS OF MORTGAGE BORROWING

The qualify for a mortgage—and to operate as a true Power Borrower in dealings with your banker—it's necessary for you to meet certain financial standards. I think of these in terms of several "basics" that characterize the most effective mortgage borrowing.

Basic # 1: Establish a long-term
relationship with a bank

There is no set amount of time that you must be with a bank to be regarded as a "long-term," or "favored," or "priority" customer. But certainly, I think you should be a substantial customer for at least six months, and preferably for several years.

On the other hand, if you only keep a small balance in your bank accounts—say an average of a couple of hundred dollars—that won't help much, even if you've been with a particular bank for a number of years. It's best to do most or all your business with one bank so that you can demonstrate a substantial business relationship. Then, when you apply for a mortgage with that bank, you'll be more likely to get approval of your application, and perhaps even a better deal on interest rates or fees.

Basic # 2: Demonstrate job stability

Even more important than a long-term relationship with a bank is your job history. Most banks will take on any new customer who can show a solid record of job stability. It's not that changing your job every so often is a bad thing. But the person who changes jobs frequently — or worse, shifts back and forth often among different occupational fields—isn't regarded as a sound mortgage risk.

According to one major New York bank, successful loan applicants should have been employed in the same line of work—though not necessarily in the same job—for at least two years prior to their application. Many other lending institutions have similar policies.

How about self-employed people? They are in a special situation with regard to mortgages, and the first attitude of a lender evaluating a loan application may be negative. There may be a particular problem with self-employed people who gross a lot of money, but take home a relatively small amount as a salary. As one banker says, "A self-employed person in this situation can't have his cake and eat it too."

Self-employed people have an advantage in being able to write off expenses on their tax returns that salaried people can't deduct. These write-offs can keep the gross personal income of a self-employed individual relatively low, at least on paper. One beneficial result of the extra deductions is to reduce the income taxes this person has to pay.

But banks won't give a self-employed individual any special breaks for this advantage they have on their tax returns. For purposes of a mortgage application, the salary of self-employed people is taken to be what they report as adjusted gross income to the Internal Revenue Service—*not* what their gross business receipts may be, before all those write-offs.

Still, self-employed people may get special breaks with certain banks if they're willing to make a larger down payment. One large bank will accept the self-employed person's income as that person states it—*if* the person is willing to make a larger down payment than normal. Typically, in this situation this bank wants down payments of 25 percent or more of the asking price of the property.

Basic # 3: Be able to show adequate net personal assets, including an ability to make a 20-percent down payment

Bankers like to see financial discipline, including an ability to save. One reason is that they are especially interested in identifying the personal funds from which the down payment for the property will come.

I realize that it's quite possible to make a lower down payment, say of 10 percent or in some cases even 5 percent of the purchase price. But the standard expectation is to make a down payment of 20 percent of the purchase price, and I'd advise you to make that your objective. Not only will you impress a banker more with larger assets on hand, but you might be able to get a more attractive arrangement on your interest rate or payment of "points."

Basic # 4: Have a good credit rating

Every banker who evaluates a mortgage applicant will check the person's credit record with TRW or one of the other credit bureaus. The standards for approval for a mortgage application are at least as stringent as those for getting any other sort of credit or loan. So be sure you have a good credit history. If you've gotten into the habit of making late payments on your credit cards or being delinquent with loans, you'll be in a much more difficult position when you apply for a mortgage.

On the other hand, there are some exceptions to the traditional requirement for a solid credit rating. For example, many bankers in large urban areas know that some recent immigrants tend to have no credit rating or record, even though they're financially quite stable. The reason for this is that members of these groups, while financially responsible, often have a tradition of never borrowing money.

The experienced loan officer will take facts like these into account and may overlook the lack of a credit record when they're evaluating these particular mortgage applications.

Basic # 5: Avoid having too many credit lines

Having a number of large credit lines may work against you in applying for a mortgage. When a banker — especially a more conservative one — considers you for a mortgage, he will most likely assume that you'll be using *all* your credit lines, to the maximum once you own the house.

Suppose, for instance, you have a $5,000 credit line on

your MasterCard and a $10,000 check overdraft line, but you've only used a total of $2,000 of those lines. The banker will still assume that you've used or could use the total $15,000 of your credit when he's evaluating you for a mortgage.

What this all means, in very practical, dollars-and-cents terms, is that the banker will disregard how much credit you're *actually* using and focus instead on the maximum you are *entitled* to use. Then, he will add the total of the maximum possible amounts of all your credit lines to determine what he would expect you to be able to pay on your monthly mortgage. The more credit lines you have, the smaller the mortgage you can qualify for with many banks.

Bankers assume, by the way, that it will take sixty months, or five years, to pay off any credit line. So, if you have a credit line of $12,000 that you can draw upon, the banker would divide that by 60 to get a total monthly payment of $200. Then, if your gross salary is $4,000 per month, your credit line will represent 5 percent of that figure.

What lesson should we take away from Basic # 5? Simply that it may be wise to get rid of some of your credit lines a year or so before you plan to apply for a mortgage. That way, it will be clearer to your banker that you are likely to have fewer nonmortgage debt obligations.

Basic # 6: Observe the 28–34 rule

Many bankers seriously abide by this rule that states that mortgage payments, including real estate taxes, should amount to no more than 28 percent of a person's gross salary per month. Furthermore, when the mortgage payments are added in, a person should be spending no more than 34 percent of his gross salary per month to service all his debts.

As an illustration, assume you can get a mortgage equal to 28 percent of your gross salary. In that case, your other debt service—including the maximum amount of all your outstanding credit lines — cannot amount to more than 6 percent of your gross salary.

Why is this? It's a matter of simple arithmetic because 28 percent plus 6 percent equals 34 percent, or the maximum allowable percentage of gross salary for debt service.

This rule justifies the importance of keeping your total maximum credit lines low, as we saw under Basic # 5. Suppose you're not using all your available credit, but you still have access to credit lines that represent a substantial percentage of your gross salary. In such a case, the amount of mortgage money you can qualify for will shrink significantly.

Now, with these basics in mind, let's take a closer look at some of the different mortgages that are available.

TYPES AND TERMS OF REGULAR MORTGAGES

I've already mentioned some of the types of regular mortgages, such as fixed-rate and variable-rate loans. But more needs to be said about these and other types of loans and also special contractual terms you may encounter when you prepare to borrow on your real estate.

Fixed-rate mortgages. Fixed-rate mortgages appeal to many people—like myself—because the interest rate stays the same through the entire term of the loan. If the rate is 11 percent in the first year, it will still be 11 percent in the twentieth or thirtieth year. Your payments, which are usually made monthly, will be the same dollar amount from beginning to end. The only way the monthly or annual payments for your property might increase would be if your taxes increase.

It's a very personal question as to whether or not you should go with a fixed-rate mortgage. If you're conservative and cautious like me, a fixed-rate instrument may be necessary for your ongoing peace of mind. But that doesn't mean fixed rates are for everybody.

If you are a person who watches the interest markets closely and you're fairly confident that interest rates won't go up and will probably go down, you may want to try a variable-rate mortgage, which we'll discuss more fully in just a few moments. On the other hand, if you believe that interest rates are at a low point and will most likely go up over the long term, then you may want to apply for a fixed-rate loan, which will end up with lower rates over the next few years.

In general, you might keep in mind that mortgage rates have rarely gone above 17 percent or even stayed at that level for long. Usually, they have been lower. So it might not make sense to get a fixed-rate mortgage at or near the 17-percent level—though again, your decision here depends on your personal reading of the interest market.

Variable-rate mortgages. These loans—which also go under the name of "adjustable-rate mortgages" (ARMs) or "adjustable-rate loans"—are characterized by one key feature: Their interest rate changes periodically throughout the life of the loan, according to the movement of some outside interest rate like the prime rate.

This characteristic is extremely important because if the interest rate on your loan changes, that has a direct effect on the amount of your monthly payments. A variable-rate mortgage can provide a substantial benefit: If the loan rate goes down, you have more money available for your daily living. On the other hand, if the rate goes up, you have less available because more of your cash is going to pay for your real estate.

The changes in monthly payments can be significant, as you can see from the following example:

Suppose you get a variable-rate loan for $50,000 over a thirty-year term, with an initial rate of 13 percent. At the 13-percent rate, your monthly payment would be $553.10. But now, suppose that after the first year, the rate is adjusted up to 15 percent and after the second up to 17 percent. A 4-percent increase in your interest rate might not seem that much at first glance. But at the 17-percent rate, your payment will soar to $711.54 a month! That's over $150 per month more than you've been paying.

Even a 1-percent change in the interest payable on a variable-rate loan can deliver a solid sock to your cash flow. Here are some figures supplied by the New York State Banking Department, which show the dollar results of a 1-percent change on monthly payments. We're assuming here that the initial interest rates on the loan ranged between 10 percent and 20 percent.

RISE OR DECLINE IN MONTHLY PAYMENTS CAUSED BY
A 1-PERCENT CHANGE IN MORTGAGE RATES

Loan Amount	Term of Loan		
	20 Years	*25 years*	*30 years*
$40,000	$26–32 rise or decline	$28–32 rise or decline	$29–33 rise or decline
$60,000	39–47 rise or decline	42–49 rise or decline	44–49 rise or decline
$70,000	46–55 rise or decline	49–57 rise or decline	51–58 rise or decline

As you can see, the cost of even a 1-percent change upward in a variable-rate loan can quickly begin to add up. On the other hand, the savings can be great if interest rates go down.

If you decide to go the variable-rate route, here are some questions you should be prepared to ask your lender:

- *What is the adjustment period?* For most variable-rate instruments, the changes in rate can be made only after the end of an "adjustment period," which is one of many equal time frames into which the loan is divided. The contract may call for possible adjustments at the end of every six months or at the end of every five years. Most commonly, adjustment periods run for six months or one year.

- *What is the rate index?* The interest rate on a variable-rate loan is always based on some outside economic index, such as the prime rate or the rates of six-month or one-year treasury bills. The loan rate and the index rate move up and down together, though the loan rate is always higher than the index rate because the lender will add a set margin of 1 percent, 2 percent, or more to the index rate.

   In certain economic climates, some rates tend to be more volatile than others; so it's wise to investigate how your lender's index responds to various economic conditions. In any event, you should ask your lender to show you how his or her index has performed during the past ten years or so.

- *Is there a rate "cap"?* Some variable-rate loans provide for limits or "caps" on rate increases and decreases, even though movements in the index might call for greater rate changes. For more cautious borrowers, such a cap can afford a midway approach between the unlimited variable-rate mortgage and the completely predictable fixed-rate type.

Here's how a 2-percent cap might work: Assume you get a $60,000, thirty-year variable-rate loan at 13.5 percent, with a 2-percent cap per adjustment period and a 3-percent "lifetime cap." Your adjustment periods for this loan are one year each.

This loan would begin with monthly payments of $687.25, and would remain constant throughout the first year. But then, if the loan index rises sharply—say 3 percent—your adjustment period cap of 2 percent would hold your interest rate at 15.5 percent. Your loan payments at this rate would be $782.71 monthly.

Now, assume that rates in the economy continue to skyrocket, going up 2 percent, 4 percent, or even more. Your interest payments would be capped at the 3-percent lifetime cap, or 16.5 percent. At that level, your monthly loan payments would hold steady at $831.09.

With this cap approach, you still run the risk of facing higher monthly payments. But at least there is a limit on how much extra money you'll have to come up with. Also, remember this: If the cap applies to rate decreases, you could end up losing some of the benefits of a variable-rate mortgage in a situation where interest rates are declining significantly.

Caution: Be sure that you distinguish between (1) an ordinary variable-rate loan with a cap on rate increases, of the type that we've been discussing, and (2) a capped-payment variable-rate mortgage that involves *negative amortization of interest*.

With this latter type of cap, you may pay lower monthly payments for a while. But what will also be happening is that the increased interest on the loan will accumulate, and you'll have to pay that interest later, probably in the form of a huge increase in monthly payments.

Here's how this might work: Suppose you take out a $50,000, twenty-five-year variable-rate mortgage, with an initial interest rate of 13 percent. The interest is adjusted yearly, and the increase in your monthly payments is "capped" for three years.

At the beginning, your monthly payment would be $563.92. But then, assume that interest rates rise, and the rate of your loan increases to 15 percent at the end of the first year, to 16 percent at the end of the second year, and to 17 percent at the end of the third year. During those first three years your monthly payment will stay at $563.92. But at the start of the fourth year, the monthly payment will increase by nearly $200.

The reason for this is that you didn't have to pay the increased interest immediately in your monthly payments during those first three years. But the interest accumulated to increase your total loan amount from $50,000 to $51,862—and now, you're making monthly payments on that larger sum.

So be sure you understand what your lender means if he says the loan involves a "cap."

Don't jump too quickly toward "discounts"! Some variable-rate mortgages are offered at very low beginning rates—say 2 percent or more below current rates for other variable-rate loans. But problems may lurk behind this attractive facade.

Typically, the low introductory or discounted rate will continue only until the first rate adjustment, which usually occurs after one year. If there is no cap on rate adjustments after that, the rate on your loan could jump above other variable-rate instruments. So if you decide to go with this type of loan, be sure you have an appropriate cap.

In any event, it's important not to be swayed by the attractive initial rate. Always ask about the full rate for the loan—the index rate plus the margin—and compare that with rates for other variable-rate mortgages. If the full rate is much higher than that for other nondiscounted mortgages, it will be wise for you to forget the discount, which isn't really a discount at all.

Beware of balloons! Balloon loans are offered for short terms, usually one to five years. Then, they are repaid as though they were long-term loans, perhaps with a payment schedule of thirty years.

As you'll recall, a benefit of a balloon loan is that the initial rate is usually quite attractive. That can be helpful for families and individuals who will be financially strapped unless they can start out with relatively low monthly payments. But like all other variable-rate mortgages, the possibility is there that rates will increase. Also, these loans have to be refinanced several times during the lengthy repayment period. This means that the mortgage has to be renegotiated, with a new set of initial payments, such as closing costs. At the beginning of each of those refinancing periods, the interest rate may soar. In addition, the increase in rates won't be limited by an index calculation, but instead will be determined by the lender's subjective determination of what the market will bear.

And there are other potential problems: At each refinancing, you'll have to pay extra legal costs, title insurance expenses, and other fees, just as you did when you first took out the loan. Finally, if your lender doesn't agree to refinance at the beginning of one of the refinancing periods — or if you don't want to accept his terms—you have a difficult choice: Either you go to another lender and take out another loan, with all the attendant expenses. Or you pay off the balance of the amount due on your balloon loan.

My advice: Stay away from balloons!

There are other ways that the Power Borrower can get involved with taking out loans on his or her property. Suppose you want to get some additional money for investment or educational purposes. One way to turn your house into a ready source of cash is the home equity loan.

YOUR HOUSE AS A CASH COW

One of the most popular sources of personal borrowing on real estate in recent years has been the home equity loan—which is, in effect, a second mortgage with relatively flexible terms for obtaining cash.

The regular second mortgage usually involves a fixed-rate or standard variable-rate arrangement, where you get a loan in a lump sum. Then, you make monthly payments on the total amount of the loan until it's repaid.

In contrast, the home equity loan is a revolving-credit arrangement with a variable interest rate. Also, repayment schedules can often be set up to meet a borrower's special needs. For example, in the first part of the loan period, you maybe want to pay only the interest that is due. Then, you can pay the principal later as part of a much larger set of payments.

Once you've set up your home equity account, you can draw on it as you need the money by using a special credit card or special checks. After you repay part of the balance due, you can then borrow that amount again.

In addition to providing a relatively large pool of funds for borrowing, a home equity loan also has a number of tax advantages. You can deduct interest payments on a home equity loan up to the original purchase price of your home, plus the cost of any home improvements (and minus the cost of your first mortgage balance). If you borrow amounts on a home equity loan beyond these limits, interest may still be written off if the funds are used for home improvements, or for educational or medical purposes.

Some other facts about home equity loans:

• Currently, you pay about 1.75 percent above the prime lending rate, and this amount can rise or fall, depending on general interest-rate movements.

• There are a number of expenses connected with home equity loans, such as appraisals, title searches, attorney's fees, credit checks, and origination fees or "points." These may vary up to $2,000 or more. So most experts advise borrowers to forget this type of loan unless they plan to borrow a sizable amount of money.

• The amount you can borrow is limited by the outstanding equity in your home. Right now, many banks will lend up to 80 to 90 percent of the fair market value of your house, minus the outstanding principal on your mortgage. So, if you have a $200,000 home and $100,000 outstanding on the principal of your mortgage, you could borrow up to $80,000.

- Your credit line *won't* increase if the value of your property increases. When you apply for a home equity loan, that sets the size of your credit line. If you want to increase your borrowing power based on the increased value of your property, you'll have to take out another home equity loan—with all the attendant costs.

The home equity loan is in many ways an extremely attractive source of credit for those who own a house. But there are a number of possible traps that can snare the unwary borrower who plunges into this approach without first laying down a sound strategy. The Power Borrower who is considering the home equity route to taking out a loan should always keep in mind the following home equity guidelines, which I recommend to all my clients.

Guideline # 1: All the sound borrowing principles that apply to other loans also apply to home equity.

This means that you should be sure that you're on solid ground with such issues as your personal budget and that you observe the "commandments" of Power Borrowing discussed in Chapter 2. Home equity loans are just another type of loan; they don't involve a separate set of rules or behaviors.

Guideline # 2: Use money you borrow on a home equity loan only for making investments.

Under no circumstances should the Power Borrower use funds from a home equity loan for daily living expenses, personal entertainment, or vacations. If you do that, you'll be depleting an asset—i.e., your real estate. On the other hand, if you use the money for investments, you'll be *leveraging* your real estate holdings to increase the size of your total portfolio.

One young childless couple had a gross annual family income of $75,000. Because their living expenses were relatively low, they found they were able to save 10 percent of their take-home pay each year. At the same time, they felt quite comfortable making payments on a $150,000 home.

When their personal savings had risen to a total of about $30,000, they decided that they would invest $20,000 of the money in a rental real estate venture and put another $20,000 into this investment from a home equity loan. You'll note that with $10,000 still remaining in their savings account, they followed the rule of having at least 50 percent of their outstanding loan balance in liquid savings.

They were able to leverage — or multiply—their investments through intelligent borrowing. At the same time, by backing their loan by at least 50 percent in liquid savings, they were in a position to continue to make loan payments if they encountered a temporary interruption in their cash flow. In a sense, they enjoyed a kind of "double security" in that their loan was backed both by their real estate _and_ by their savings accounts.

Furthermore, the fact that they were borrowing through a home equity loan meant that (1) they were getting a lower interest rate than if they had taken out an unsecured line of credit, and (2) they could deduct the interest on the home equity loan from their income tax.

On the other hand, I've also encountered a number of families who are under much more financial pressure, and they resort to a home equity loan for daily living expenses. This approach to borrowing is a slippery slope that is almost certain to increase the financial pressure on those families at some point in the future. Not that many houses with home equity loans become subject to foreclosure proceedings by the lenders because of a failure to pay. But the danger of this result increases when home equity funds are used for personal living expenses.

Another danger area on the home equity scene is the retired person. Sometimes, those who have paid off their homes may be tempted to take out a home equity mortgage to get some extra cash. In almost every case, I would say,

"Don't!" It's too important for most retired people to have the peace of mind knowing that their shelter is secure for the rest of their lives. Of course, there may be some exceptions, as with those who own two homes. But in general, I'd reiterate: "Don't!"

To sum up then, the only wise use of a home equity loan for most people is to use the money for investments. The only legitimate exception I can think of would be to draw on these funds for medical emergencies or for educational expenses. Sometimes, you may feel you simply have to get a substantial amount of extra cash to pay heavy hospital bills for a loved one, or to give a child a once-in-a-lifetime opportunity to go to an excellent, but expensive college.

But even in these cases, I'd usually recommend that you try other types of borrowing or other sources of funds before you put your property under a second mortgage. As serious and worthwhile as medical and educational expenses may seem, they will still deplete the value of your property through a mortgage: Your equity, or degree of ownership in the property, will decline in direct proportion to the amount of debt on the real estate.

Guideline # 3: Keep in mind all the advice and warnings you've received about other types of mortgages.

Everything I've said about such issues as fixed versus variable rates, balloons, discounted deals, and "caps" applies to home equity mortgages, too. Just as you don't leave your basic borrowing principles behind when you enter the world of home equity financing, you shouldn't forget what you know in general about mortgages, either.

A MIXED BAG OF MORTGAGE TIPS

In the years that I've spent advising various clients about their borrowing practices, I've collected a "mixed bag" of tips about mortgages. You may find some of these to be helpful as a partial checklist when you're exploring mortgages, home equity loans or similar borrowing vehicles.

Tip # 1: Watch for "escape clauses" that allow lenders to get out of low interest rates they have offered in loan applications.

Typically, the lender will include a clause, often on the back of the loan application form, saying that it has the right to change the offered interest rate under some circumstances. Some federal and state agencies are taking steps to restrict this practice, but as of now, it's still going on. So be careful and read your loan papers closely.

Tip # 2: Beware of come-on ads for low-cost home loans.

In many cases, the low initial rates are just a front for later increases. Again, take a close look at the terms of any contracts you sign.

Tip # 3: Some lenders may offer special breaks to two-career couples who are relocating.

The key here is to find a lender who will count the salaries of _both_ spouses, even though one may have been left temporarily jobless as a result of a relocation move. Some lenders still follow the practice of looking only at the spouse with the highest income. But that attitude is changing — especially in those cases where the jobless spouse works in a field where his or her services are in demand, such as nursing. The trick is to find a lender who is more up-to-date in his understanding of the situation of two-career couples.

Still, even many of the forward-looking lenders are cautious in the terms they impose on these couples. For example, they may require that these husbands and wives put in escrow an amount equal to six months of mortgage payments. This deposit will be returned when the jobless spouse has finally found work.

Tip # 4: Some retired people may want to consider donations of homes or "creative" financing to increase their income.

I've already cautioned that it's often unwise for retired people to get involved in an ordinary home equity loan to increase their ready cash. But there are some alternative approaches to using their real estate that may prove more attractive.

For example, some older people have decided to donate their homes to charities or educational institutions in exchange for a lifetime annuity. These arrangements allow the householder to retain a "life estate" in the property, so that he can remain in the house until he dies. After that, the property passes on to the institution to which it was donated.

One California widow, for example, donated her $200,000 home to the University of California at Los Angeles in exchange for a lifetime annuity of $8,000 a year and also a large tax deduction. She has the right to live in the house until she dies, and at that time, UCLA will get it.

In addition to such donations, the older person may want to consider a "reverse mortgage" to a lender. In this arrangement, the lending institution pays the homeowner monthly loan amounts. When the term of the loan is up, the homeowner must then pay the principal and interest—a payment that is usually accomplished by selling the home. If the owner dies or sells the house before the term of the loan is up, the loan principal and interest come due.

As with the home equity situation, it's important for older people considering options like these to examine their contracts closely with the help of a qualified attorney. Think through every aspect of the transaction — especially the emotional impact of losing part or all of the rights to your home. If you don't feel comfortable with such an arrangement, then you shouldn't get involved in a deal like this.

Also, it's essential to be certain that the organizations you're dealing with are solid and experienced in the sort of transaction you're considering. For example, if you're going to donate your property, it's important to be sure that the charity or educational institution is fiscally responsible and based on a solid financial footing. If the organization goes out of business shortly after you've made your new property arrangement, you could find yourself stuck in a morass of legal complications.

Tip # 5: Before you consider refinancing your mortgage, try negotiating a simple amendment with your lender.

When interest rates fall, many homeowners start thinking about refinancing their old mortgages at the newer, lower rates. But then, when they learn that a series of fees will be involved—such as new appraisals, credit checks, title searches, and attorney's costs—they back off.

But don't run away too quickly. It may be possible to avoid refinancing entirely by talking to your lender and getting him to amend the old mortgage to give you a lower interest rate. Many lenders are willing to take this approach to avoid losing the borrower's business to another bank or financial institution.

Tip # 6: If you run into problems getting a loan, ask your real estate broker for some "creative" assistance.

Many times, the delays in obtaining loans can blow deals for brokers and for prospective buyers. But if a borrower just mentions the problem to a broker and asks for help, he may be surprised at the response.

In some recent markets, brokers have been willing to buy a home themselves on an interim basis, until the buyer's financing came through. One in Milwaukee recently owned a home for about a week until the buyer could close. "The carrying cost was three hundred dollars, but we covered our costs," the broker said.

Obviously, this is an unusual step for a broker to take—and potentially a risky one. But with the proper legal paperwork, everyone can receive reasonable protection, and a difficult real estate deal can be made much easier.

Tip # 7: When the time comes to make the final payment on a mortgage, don't let the euphoria you feel obscure the need to be careful about the final paperwork.

In making the final payment on a mortgage, borrowers may make important errors that can create problems when the homes are being refinanced or offered for sale. Some of these errors include the following:

- Not doing the paperwork necessary to be sure that a release from a mortgage is indicated on the deed

- Failing to keep documents that prove the mortgage was actually paid off

- Planning inadequately to pay for real estate taxes and homeowner's insurance premiums, which were previously paid by the lending institution

Tip # 8: Know all the implications if you decide to prepay the mortgage.

Sometimes, it can make a lot of sense to prepay a mortgage — or pay the balance of the loan before it comes due. For example, with lower tax rates, the tax deductions for a mortgage are currently worth less than they were in the past. Also, prepaying can save a tremendous amount in interest.

Assume that you have a $150,000 mortgage at a 10-percent interest rate for thirty years, with a monthly payment of $1,316.36. The total cost of the mortgage will be $473,889.60—and that includes $323,883.14 in interest.

But if you pay only $100 extra each month, over the thirty-year term of the loan, that additional payment could reduce your total interest outlays to $215,523.79—a savings of more than $100,000! Furthermore, the more you prepay, the more you'll be able to save in interest.

On the other hand, before you make plans to repay — or better yet, before you sign your mortgage agreement in the first place—it's important to check any prepayment penalty that your lender may require. If you have a mortgage from a federally chartered financial institution, there may be prepayment penalties. So if you get your loan from a federal savings and loan association or federal savings bank, be sure to check for this provision.

On the other hand, many state-chartered banks have strict limits on prepayment penalties. In New York, for instance, a fee can be charged on a fixed-rate mortgage only if the loan is repaid within the first year of its term — *and* if the contract provides for such a fee. For variable-rate mortgages, no prepayment penalties are allowed unless the interest rate stays the same for five years.

I HAVE A LITTLE LIST . . .

Here's a nonmortgage, nonloan checklist that should help you in making a decision about any house you may want to purchase. It's important for every prospective mortgage holder to have a little list like this as an adjunct to the various checklists he or she may compile in dealing with a lending institution.

I've included points under this list that have been important to me in my own house-hunting. You'll most likely want to adjust some of the specifics to your own needs.

1. Location
   Not too isolated
   Easy access to recreation, such as tennis courts

Town road (suitable for bicycling)—not a highway

Neighboring properties selling at the same or higher market value

Proximity to town

Proximity to train or bus

Desirable town

2. Aesthetics

Exterior pleasing to look at

Feeling of daylight throughout interior

3. Quality

Tightness of house (heat efficiency)

Solid materials, workmanship

Hardwood floors

Wood clapboard, brick, cedar shingle, or stucco siding

Andersonlike storm windows, doors

Safe and efficient wiring

Solid walls, ceilings

4. Kitchen

Ample for group cooking, "hanging out"

Eat-in kitchen, with view of backyard, birds

Appliances (refrigerator, oven) included

Sufficient counter space or possibility for center aisle

Lighting

5. Bathrooms

New, modern fixtures

At least one and a half baths

Strong water pressure

6. Storage/closeting

Place for garden tools, bikes, skis

Linen/towel closet near bedrooms

Equivalent of attic
Garage

7. Den or equivalent for office

8. Inside/outside
Porch, patio, and/or deck
Good views of grounds from major rooms
(living room, den, kitchen)

9. Gardening/land
Potential for vegetable garden
Potential for country garden
Space for forsythia, lilacs
Mature trees
Space for game court (croquet, badminton, catch)
Safe for pet cat
Possibility of hammock/swing

10. Items and areas that need to be fixed
In first three. months. Amount:
In first year. Amount:
In first three years. Amount:

11. Maintenance costs
Real estate taxes:
Heat:
Water:
Electric:
Rubbish:
Gardening:

12. Miscellaneous
Dampness of cellar, drainage implications
Zoning
Other:

CHAPTER 10

It's a New Tax Game

As a result of recent changes in the federal tax laws, the rules of the "borrowing game" have changed.

Before the new tax laws, borrowing under a variety of circumstances often seemed attractive because of the broad opportunities to deduct interest payments on income tax returns. But the latest reforms have eliminated many of these interest deductions—and with them, much of the motivation to borrow.

Of course, tax laws change frequently as new legislatures and new presidential administrations come into office. So there's no guarantee that current laws will stay the same forever. In fact, you could say there's a guarantee that they *won't* stay the same.

Still, there does seem to be deep-rooted sentiment for wiping out many of the deductions that well-heeled, high-income tax itemizers have used in the past to reduce their tax obligations. An estimated 28 percent of households were claiming interest deductions before 1986, when tax reform legislation was passed. But that figure is likely to drop considerably because the opportunities for interest deductions have been virtually eliminated in a number of areas.

A broad-based, egalitarian-oriented consumer tax reform movement seems firmly set on eliminating many of the "write-offs" that provided shelters of tax-free income for the well-off. And one of the most attractive of those tax deductions—a deduction that has now largely gone the way of the dodo bird—was interest paid on debt.

In general, our federal tax laws currently provide the following with regard to personal debt and interest deductions:

- A gradual elimination of the tax deduction for consumer debt and personal loans, until the deduction disappears entirely after 1990. The deductions prohibited include interest on loans for cars, vacations, and educational loans. Also, deductions are being phased out for interest payments on credit card purchases and similar personal interest payments.

- A gradual elimination of the tax deduction for interest over net investment income that is paid "on margin" to buy investments—until there is no deduction for interest in excess of investment income after 1990.

- Mortgage interest deductions can only be claimed for two houses. Furthermore, there are strict limits on how much can be deducted for those two houses.

- A ceiling on the interest that can be deducted for home equity loans.

- Reduced opportunities for tax breaks from the remaining interest deductions and other write-offs because lower tax rates have made the savings through tax deductions less valuable.

Assume, for example, that you can still take a certain interest deduction that was also available under the old tax law, such as a deduction for mortgage payments on your home. Also, assume that the deduction has been $4,000 annually over the years and that you have consistently been in the top income tax bracket.

Under the old law you would have received a 50-percent reduction in your tax bill, or a reduction of about $2,000. Under current law, however, with a top tax bracket of 28 percent, the deduction would only be worth a little more than $1,100.

To understand better how some of these changes can affect your approach to borrowing, let's take a closer look now at some of the details of these new rules.

WHY CONSUMER INTEREST IS LESS INTERESTING

As I've said, the new tax law has provided for a gradual elimination of the deduction of interest payments made on consumer debt (including credit card charges) and on personal loans. Specifically, the rules make these provisions:

• In the 1987 tax year, you were able to deduct 65 percent of your personal interest payments.

• For 1988, the law provided for a deduction of 40 percent.

• For 1989, you can write off 20 percent of your interest.

• For the 1990 tax year, you can deduct 10 percent.

• After 1990, you won't be able to deduct any personal interest expenses at all.

What should be your personal borrowing strategy in light of these changes in the law?

The smartest approach is to arrange your finances so that you pay as little as possible in interest on personal consumer loans or credit card installment debts. If you make purchases with a credit card, pay the entire bill within the designated grace period, before you incur any interest charges. Also, it would be wise to eliminate the number of credit cards you hold to cut the yearly fees you pay and also to reduce the temptation to rely on debt.

In fact, a study of consumers conducted by Payment Systems, Inc. and reported in the *American Banker* (April 27, 1987) revealed that many well-to-do individuals planned to reduce their personal debt levels *and* reduce the number of credit cards they held.

For example, of people under forty years of age, making $35,000 to $50,000 annually, 59 percent said they planned to reduce their personal debt levels and 43 percent intended to reduce their number of credit cards. Among those under forty years of age making more than $50,000 annually, 55 percent stated they planned to reduce their debts and 33 percent planned to reduce their number of credit cards.

Middle-aged, middle-income family people—ranging from forty to fifty years of age and from $35,000 to $50,000 in income—indicated they felt the strongest of any group about the issue: 64 percent stated they would reduce their debt levels with the new tax law, and 47 percent declared they would reduce the number of credit cards they held.

Of those aged 40 to 65 making more than $50,000 a year, 50 percent said they planned to reduce debt levels and 34 percent said they would reduce their credit cards.

Of course, as the full impact of the current tax reforms are felt, it remains to be seen whether these consumers will live up to their stated intentions. One report from the Federal Reserve Board in early 1988 showed that installment credit was definitely on the rise. Debt as a percentage of disposable income moved up to an all-time high of 18.8 percent in the first quarter of 1988!

Those who hope to be Power Borrowers should make every effort to eliminate their payments for personal interest. If you use credit cards, you should pay your bills in full when they come due and not allow interest charges to accumulate.

Outlays on personal debt are now money down the drain and can only work against your objective of becoming financially strong and independent.

THE REAL ESTATE SNARE

Interest paid on many real estate loans continues to be deductible on personal income tax returns. But there are still plenty of snares that may throw the unwary borrower for a financial loss. Here are some important rules that should help you avoid various real estate borrowing traps.

The Two-Residence Rule

In general, mortgage interest paid on a first home and second home are deductible (with the qualifications discussed below). But mortgage interest on additional homes or other real estate holdings is not deductible — except as a personal interest deduction, which will be completely phased out after 1990.

Note: Additional real estate you own as an investment, such as rental property, may qualify you for certain interest deductions. But there are strict limits: For investments in real estate made after the new tax law went into effect (October 22, 1986), interest paid can only be deducted up to the amount of income earned. Any interest payments that exceed income must be carried forward to offset income in later years, or to reduce taxes when the property is finally sold.

On the other hand, real estate investors who *actively* manage their properties can get an additional tax break: Those with adjusted gross incomes below $100,000 can use any losses above income from the real estate to offset income from any source up to $25,000. But this $25,000 cap gradually decreases until there is no extra write-off on taxes for those having adjusted gross incomes above $150,000.

The Cost-Plus-Improvements Rule

The loan interest on a first or second home can still be fully deductible if the borrower meets certain strict requirements.

Specifically, the amount of the loan taken out after August 16, 1986, must not exceed the purchase price of the home, plus the cost of any improvements made on the home. If the loan is greater than the purchase price of the house plus the cost of improvements, the interest attributable to the excess amount of the loan is only deductible under two possible circumstances: if the loan is used for either medical or educational expenses.

To illustrate, suppose you bought a house twenty-five years ago for $25,000, but now it's worth $225,000. If you take out a mortgage on this property, how much of the interest could you deduct?

You can only write off the interest on the original purchase price of $25,000, according to the new law. The only exceptions would be

1. If you made improvements to the property, which would allow you additional interest deductions on the loan up to the amount of the improvements.

2. If you used the loan to pay for educational or medical expenses.

Take another example: Suppose you bought your home for $60,000 a number of years ago and added $40,000 in improvements, including an extra wing on the house. Your home is now worth well over $175,000, and so you decide to take out a home equity loan of $110,000. How much of the interest on that loan will be deductible?

Under the new tax law, you can deduct the interest on $100,000 of the loan (an amount equal to the $60,000 purchase price of the home, plus the $40,000 in improvements). But you can't deduct the interest on the extra $10,000 of the loan—unless you've spent the loan for education or medical purposes.

The Educational and Medical Expense Rule

What constitutes an "educational" or "medical" purpose under the new mortgage-deduction provisions?

Medical expenses that will qualify you for the deduction include unreimbursed expenses for medical care of the taxpayer, the taxpayer's spouse, or the taxpayer's dependents.

Educational expenses that qualify include tuition payments, away-from-home living expenses for students in the family from the lowest elementary school grades to graduate school.

But both the medical and educational expenses must be "paid or incurred within a reasonable period of time before or after such indebtedness is incurred," according to the tax law. So, if you take out a second mortgage or home equity loan and immediately write out a check for this year's expenses, you'd certainly qualify for the interest deduction on your loan. But if you wait several years to pay those educational or medical expenses, you may not qualify for the interest deduction.

How should these facts about home loans influence the personal financial strategy of the Power Borrower?

Here is one possibility: If you bought your home years ago at a price far below what it's now worth, you might consider selling it and buying another to increase your cost basis and borrowing power.

For example, if you paid $25,000 for your home and it's now worth $225,000, you can only write off the interest on a new mortgage or home equity loan up to $25,000—unless you've used the loan for educational or medical purposes. But if you sell your home and buy another for $225,000, you can then write off the interest on a loan up to the full $225,000 purchase price—with no strings attached.

As a matter of fact, Internal Revenue Commissioner Lawrence B. Gibbs predicted, in an interview in *The New York Times* (October 28, 1986), that increasing numbers of homeowners would be encouraged to sell their old homes and buy new ones to increase their borrowing power. I imagine that if a person is on the fence about buying a new home, this significant tax-deduction consideration could easily swing the balance.

Finally, even with the limits on tax deductions that some homeowners may face if they take out a loan on their house, these loans may still be considerably more attractive than anything else.

Remember: If you take out a loan to cover any personal expenses or if you purchase on time by credit card, your ability to deduct the interest on those loans or cards is now very limited. And after 1990, the deduction will disappear entirely.

In contrast, interest paid on loans on any two residences you may own is fully deductible, within the limits we've already described. So, many people are turning to their real estate to increase their borrowing power. Some borrowers, for instance, are taking out a second mortgage or home equity loan and using it to consolidate loans that require payments of nondeductible interest. They may pay off debts such as credit card obligations or unsecured bank loans, which allow no interest deductions after 1990.

FURTHER TIPS ON AVOIDING
HOME-LOAN TAX TRAPS

Although many tax considerations connected with home loans are beyond the scope of this book, I want to mention three more key tax tips. These should both help you make mortgage decisions, and also save some money in tax payments. Other nontax issues related to mortgages were dealt with in Chapter 8.

Tip # 1: Distinguish between the tax and investment benefits when you're considering a home equity loan and a second mortgage

First of all, recall the differences between home equity loans and second mortgages:

The tax advantages of these two loans are similar: You can deduct the interest on your income tax return on either type of loan—up to the purchase price of your house plus any improvements—regardless of the purposes for which you use the loan. Also, if you use the loan to pay medical or educational expenses, you can write off the interest on the amount of the loan that exceeds the purchase price of the property plus improvements.

But it's important to be cautious with both home equity loans and second mortgages. The revolving nature of many home equity loans, for example, may cause the amount of your total debt to creep up on you. Before you're aware of what's happened, you may be far over your head in debt—and the fact that you can write it off on your income tax won't be much consolation!

Also, with both home equity loans and second mortgages, the interest rates may be variable. As you already know, this means that the lender can increase them as interest rates in the financial markets increase. In fact, there may be no ceiling on just how high those rates can rise.

If interest rates rise to extremely high levels, you may find that even though the interest is tax-deductible, you can't afford the out-of-pocket costs of servicing the loan. In such a case, if you fall behind in your loan payments, your credit rating could be severely damaged. Even more serious, the lender may foreclose on your property, and you could lose your home.

The main lesson in taking out one of these home loans is this: Don't focus only on the tax benefits. Taxes are certainly one important consideration in deciding whether or not to use real estate loans for your debts. But they are only one factor. It's much more important to keep your entire financial picture in mind and to be sure that you're not in danger of paying more in servicing your debts than you can afford.

Tip # 2: Evaluate the advantages and disadvantages of short- and long-term loans

At this writing, the top personal income tax rates are considerably lower than they were two years ago. Many experts are predicting that the rates will increase again within the next few years. But there's still a chance that they will stay lower than they were in the recent past—and that may have important implications for the tax benefits of long- and short-term home loans.

In general, there will usually be significant tax benefits for those who pay off loans relatively quickly, as opposed to those who take out long-term loans. The reason for this benefit is that even though you can deduct interest on home loans on your first two residences, the deductions are worth less at higher tax rates than at lower tax rates.

For example, if your tax rate is 50 percent, as the top rate was recently, an interest deduction of $1,000 will be worth $500 in tax savings to a person in that bracket. But if your rate is only 33 percent, the interest deduction on that $1,000 interest payment will only be worth $333.

Obviously, over a period of years or even decades, the difference in tax savings can be considerable, depending on your tax rate. So a number of homeowners, who have lower tax rates and also lower tax deductions under the new law, are electing to pay off their home loans more quickly than in the past.

One study comparing fifteen-year $100,000 home loans at 9.25-percent interest, and thirty-year $100,000 home loans at 9.5-percent interest, has shown some significant differences in tax savings (*The New York Times*, January 11, 1987).

With the short-term loan, the total interest paid after fifteen years would be $85,254. Furthermore, for those in a 33-percent federal tax bracket, the after-tax net interest cost (after tax savings have been subtracted) would be $56,267.

In contrast, with the long-term thirty-year loan, the total interest paid by the end of the thirty years would be $202,708. The after-tax net interest cost would also be relatively high: $133,787.

Using slightly higher interest rates, the Federal National Mortgage Association (Fannie Mae) has compared a fifteen-year $75,000 mortgage with a fixed rate of 10 percent with a thirty-year $75,000 mortgage with a 10.5-percent rate.

The findings: The short-term mortgage involved total interest payments of $70,072, while the long-term mortgage required interest payments of $171,980. With lower tax rates, the borrowers would receive lower tax savings and pay more money out of pocket in both these cases—and the borrower with the long-term loan would be at the greater disadvantage.

But many experts warn that those borrowing on their homes shouldn't make their decisions about a short- or long-term loan only on the basis of tax considerations. The main problem with short-term home loans for many people is that the monthly costs are relatively high. Even if you're receiving significant interest savings, you may find you're having to divert too much of your disposable income to cover the costs of housing.

In many cases, then, it may be advisable for an individual or family to choose the long-term mortgage, even though the interest costs are higher and the tax benefits are less than in the past. With the lower monthly costs of a long-term loan, you'll find you have extra money to cover your other expenses and perhaps also to put into more liquid savings.

Tip # 3: Know the new rules relating to
second homes that double as rental property

In a sense, the rules on second homes that double as rental property have flip-flopped with the new law.

According to the old tax rules, owners of such property were better off if they could qualify the house as rental property, rather than as a residence. It was possible to use rental property as a broad tax shelter by writing off all property rental expenses, even when they exceeded income.

Suppose you had rental expenses of $10,000 and rental income of $8,000. Under the old law, you could write off the entire $10,000 in expenses against all sources of your income, whether they arose from the rental property or not.

But now, the write-off of rental expenses is limited to the amount of income earned. So, if you have rental expenses of $10,000 during the year but just earn rental income of $8,000, you can only write off $8,000 of those expenses.

As a result of this change, it's usually advisable from a tax viewpoint to qualify your second house as a residence, even if you rent it out for part of the year. What's the reason for this? Remember: You can't write off property rental expenses beyond the amount of your rental income. But you can still deduct mortgage interest and property taxes on a residence—even if those expenses exceed rental income. The only limits on the interest deduction are that it must arise from a loan that is no greater than the purchase price of the property plus improvements.

How do you qualify your second home as a residence, even when you rent it out? It's relatively simple. All you have to do is spend more than fourteen days in the home during the year.

WHAT ABOUT MARGIN LOANS?

Interest on margin loans—which are loans or lines of credit you get from a broker or brokerage house to buy an investment like stocks—used to be a great, low-rate source of borrowing for personal expenses. Here's how the margin loan works:

In general, you can borrow to buy stock or other investments by first establishing a "margin account" with a brokerage firm. This is simply an account that gives you the right to buy securities on credit. Then, to purchase a security on credit, you have to put up a certain percentage of the purchase price of the security.

With equities like stocks, for example, you have to pay at least 50 percent of the purchase price of the stocks, excluding broker commissions. This 50 percent is called the "initial margin requirement." The brokerage firm puts up the other 50 percent of the purchase price as a loan to you. So, if you buy $5,000 worth of stock on margin, you pay $2,500 plus commissions. The brokerage firm then lends you the other $2,500 at a relatively low interest rate.

So far, so good. But suppose the price of the stock you've bought drops below the original purchase price of $5,000? Customs among brokers vary. But it's well to keep in mind the policy of one company, which I've paraphrased as follows: "If at any time, we decide that the value of the securities have decreased or if for any other reason the collateral is no longer satisfactory to us, you will in accordance with our request (1) deliver additional collateral to us, *or* (2) reduce or repay in full the principal balance of your secured loan."

I think you get the picture: Margin loans in any form can be a risky business. Unfortunately, some borrowers may also take out these margin loans for personal expenses. In the past, it was common practice for people to use these margin accounts to take out a loan at relatively low interest from their broker, spend the money on an expensive car or a vacation, and then write off the interest on their taxes.

But that tax break has disappeared under the new law. To be sure, you can still take out a margin loan *and* you can write off the interest, but only up to the amount of investment income. Also, you're supposed to use the loans for investments—not for consumer purchases. If you use the loan proceeds to buy a car or go on a vacation, the loan interest will be treated like any other consumer interest: As you know, this means that the interest will be deductible in decreasing percentages up to 1990, and then will be nondeductible after 1990.

One suggestion for doing an end run around this rule that restricts the use of margin loans applied to consumer debt, goes like this:

Assume you decide to go out and take a vacation for $10,000. You have $50,000 in stock, but if you borrow directly against that stock to get money to finance your vacation, you'd have a limited ability to deduct the interest through 1990 (and no deduction after 1990).

So you try another route. You sell $10,000 worth of your stock and use the cash to pay for your vacation. Then, you notify your broker a few days later that you want to buy that $10,000 in stock back on margin.

As a result, you find yourself holding $50,000 in stock and a $10,000 loan—but a loan with interest that is fully deductible up to the amount of your investment income. The reason for this is that the loan has now become a means to finance investment debt, rather than personal consumer debt.

Will this strategy fly with the IRS? No one really knows at this point because tax rules and decisions on the new law are still being formulated. But on its face, this approach to the use of a margin loan seems perfectly acceptable.

Obviously, there are many possibilities for developing and protecting your borrowing power under the new tax law, and I've only touched on a few of them here. So in the last analysis, it's essential for you to be in touch with a good accountant or tax lawyer before you make any major decisions about your personal financial strategies.

The new tax rules are complicated enough as they now stand. And they are sure to change—perhaps significantly—in the next few years. So be sure you team up with a top-flight tax expert who can advise you about the best use of these and other techniques as you play the Power Borrower's tax game.

CHAPTER 11

When You Need
Funds Fast!

Sometimes, financial pressures may become overwhelming—even for a Power Borrower.

Perhaps you've failed to anticipate some extra fees or payments you need for a new home you're buying. Or your business has run into a dry period, with few clients and a trickling cash flow. Or you've lost your job and you need some money to tide you over for a time. Or you've allowed yourself to get too far into debt, and you need a quick influx of cash or a restructuring of your debt to allow you to keep your head above water.

In these or similar circumstances, you may find yourself in a position where you need funds and perhaps financial counseling fast—and it's helpful to be aware ahead of time what some of your options are. The following are just a few possibilities that can be employed in a variety of different situations. You may find one of them to be helpful with the particular challenges facing you, or just reading about them may trigger some other cash-conserving idea in your mind.

ONE WAY OUT: THE BRIDGE LOAN

The so-called "bridge loan" is most often used by those who need some quick money to cover expenses related to the purchase of a home. This instrument usually involves short-term financing to provide funds for closing costs and the down payment on a house.

This type of loan may help the buyer take fast advantage of a real estate bargain, or perhaps make a down payment on a house that's still being built: The money usually comes through in one to two weeks. As for interest rates, they are often established at the prime rate plus 1 or 2 percentage points, though some lenders charge much higher interest. There may also be relatively large closing costs for these loans.

For the most part, these bridge loans aren't easy to find. They aren't usually advertised by lenders, and in fact, very few lenders even offer them.

Most of the time, a bank or other institution will write these loans on an individual basis, and the money is usually made available through an unsecured promissory note. But in some cases, those who need these loans may be able to get them through their employers. In fact, according to a study conducted by the Runzheimer Reports on Relocation and published in *The New York Times* (November 22, 1987), about 75 percent of employers offer bridge loans to workers who are being relocated to other parts of the country.

If you need quick cash for house-buying purposes, how can you find one of these bridge loans? There are several possibilities:

- Ask your real estate broker for a reference.

- Check with your personal banker.

- If your own banker can't help, start shopping around until you find a bank that writes these instruments.

DON'T FORGET YOUR LIFE INSURANCE!

In his book *The Great Insurance Secret* (New York: William Morrow, 1988), insurance expert Sam E. Beller says, "One of the major benefits of building up the cash value in ordinary life insurance is that the savings portion of your policy becomes a kind of 'money tree' against which you can borrow at relatively low interest rates."

The key to this statement is the phrase "ordinary life insurance," because this type of policy has a savings feature connected with it. In contrast, another common type of life insurance, term insurance, is pure insurance in the sense that it only offers protection in the event of death.

If you've put enough money into an ordinary life policy to have built up some cash value, you can then borrow at will against that cash value. Should you need the money quickly, you can just notify the insurance company about the emergency situation and it's likely you'll get a check in a matter of days.

In many cases, if your policy has been in effect for six years or longer, you can qualify for a very low interest rate. Then, it's possible to repay the loan on a flexible basis—paying only the interest if you prefer.

But there are some disadvantages as far as your life insurance is concerned: In the first place, an outstanding loan will reduce the size of the insurance dividends to which you're entitled. Also, if you still have a loan on the policy outstanding at your death, your beneficiaries will only receive the face amount of the policy *minus* the remaining unpaid principal and interest of the loan.

THE FAMILY-OR-FRIEND FACTOR

Another source of ready loan funds in an emergency may be a family member or friend. But this approach to borrowing can be fraught with difficulties. While it may seem helpful to make money available to a loved one, a loan arrangement can in fact easily get in the way of a free and open relationship.

One of my clients, a young professional woman, once lent several hundred dollars to a friend, and that transaction placed an unnecessary strain on the relationship. The loan was an ominous presence whenever they got together — even though the loan itself was rarely discussed. Finally, when the loan had been paid off, the friendship returned to some semblance of normalcy.

If you must borrow from a friend or family member, be sure that you put the precise terms, interest, and repayment schedule in writing. That way, both parties will know exactly what's expected of them, and there will be less likelihood of a misunderstanding at a later date. Also, it's helpful to have a long talk together before you ever make such an arrangement in an effort to nip any possible problems before they develop.

But even with plenty of prior preparation, I'm not too optimistic about the prospects for most loans involving family and friends. From a variety of experiences, I've concluded that in general, it's best for friends not to lend to friends—it's also best for family members to not lend to one another. Instead, I'd recommend that if you find yourself in the position of wanting to lend to a friend, just assume the loan is a gift. Then, if you get it back, that will be fine. But at least you won't be worrying about it or be tempted to turn yourself into an ad hoc collection agency!

A related issue may involve the cosigning of a note. Sometimes, a lender will want another signature on a loan agreement. More often than not, the borrower will turn to a family member such as a parent, or a close friend to cosign. My advice: Don't do it! If you do cosign, the control of the debt will be out of your hands, and in the event your cosigner fails to pay his or her part of the note, you'll be liable for the whole thing.

An example of the strain that can be exerted on a

friendship occurred with two young women, quite good friends, who decided to cosign a note on a urban cooperative apartment. They arranged it so that each would pay one half of the monthly bill.

Unfortunately, one of the women was more conscientious about paying off her debts than was the other. As a result, their friendship came under a severe strain—and was probably saved only because they decided to sell their apartment and terminate their cosigned loan agreement.

THE CONSOLIDATION STRATEGY

Another set of circumstances where you may need money fast is the onslaught of a personal credit crunch. Certainly, this is not a situation that should be encountered by a Power Borrower. But for some reason—such as an interruption of your income or a failure to manage your debts well—you may find that you simply have too many obligations to meet all your payments.

One solution may be a consolidation loan. For example, you might turn to a bank for a loan at a lower interest rate than what you're facing with the credit card bills you can't pay off. By taking out one loan with the bank at that lower interest rate, you can liquidate all your other high-interest debt and perhaps put yourself in a position where you can pay off your obligations more easily.

But getting an attractive consolidation loan may not be so easy. Bankers do tend to have a negative view of borrowers who are seeking a consolidation loan to pay off other debt, and they're likely to examine these applications with a fine-tooth comb.

Remember, though, that banks are not the only source for a debt consolidation. Recently, Sallie Mae, the federal student loan organization, introduced such a product for borrowers who count a student loan among their debts. Finance companies also offer this type of loan—but watch for high rates here. If you're in credit trouble and you can get one of these loans, you may find that your financial troubles can be eased, at least temporarily.

Another possibility for consolidation of your loans in an emergency can be a home equity loan. But I hesitate even to mention this outlet because, as I've already indicated, a home equity loan shouldn't be used to pay off personal expenses. If you do use the money for this purpose, you'll be depleting a valuable asset, the amount of equity you have in your home. On the other hand, if you're facing a real financial emergency, a home equity loan is an option to consider.

THE COURT OF LAST RESORT:
CREDIT COUNSELING

Sometimes, a quick rush of cash just won't do the job, and serious financial problems persist. The ultimate destination on the fast track of Weak Borrowing is bankruptcy—a condition that may be unpleasant but at least must be mentioned, even in a book on Power Borrowing.

Bankruptcies among individuals in this country are definitely on the rise. Specifically, personal bankruptcies increased by nearly 35 percent in one recent year, and there seems to be no trend in the downward direction. Unfortunately, however, the tragedy of bankruptcy isn't limited to statistics.

One man thought that the financial pressures he was facing would finally be resolved when he declared bankruptcy. But in fact, he found he had tremendous difficulty getting back on his feet after going through this difficult process.

This man had all the classic marks of the person who had misused credit and now was paying the price: He didn't have a telephone, the only address he gave out was a post office box, and he was constantly "up against the wall" in his personal money management. He also found it very difficult to get a job and almost impossible to get loans for a business he wanted to establish.

Finally, after years of financial counseling, he managed to get his financial house in some sort of order. He sought help from a qualified credit counselor — one of the 282 nonprofit counseling services that belong to the National Foundation for Consumer Credit. (A listing of these organizations can be obtained by writing to the National Foundation for Consumer Credit, 8701 Georgia Avenue, Suite 507, Siiver Spring, Maryland 20910).

Today, this man has largely recovered from the major financial setbacks that had devastated him years before. But his case and others like it provide us all with a clear message: Always borrow only from a position of strength, and never from a position of weakness.

CHAPTER 12

You Can Be a Power Borrower!

Borrowing is definitely a two-edged sword.

As we've seen in the previous discussions, those who borrow unwisely will weaken their financial position and may eventually find themselves on a fast track to Weak Borrowing, or even bankruptcy. On the other hand, those who learn to borrow well—and observe the sound principles of using leverage and interest rates—will be well on their way to becoming Power Borrowers.

It's possible to list some of the features of the Power Borrower, and to the extent this is helpful, I've done this. You know now that a Power Borrower is one who is characterized by such traits as:

- An ability to organize and abide by a sound personal budget
- A good credit rating
- Strong credibility with lenders
- A knowledge of the different types of loans and techniques for exploiting them
- A virtuosity with credit cards

- Wisdom in dealing with lenders
- A practical understanding of the tax consequences of different types of borrowing
- An awareness of the pitfalls of credit that can quickly turn a Power Borrower into a Weak Borrower

All of this may seem to suggest that to become a Power Borrower you have to have a graduate degree in economics and finance—and be a practical money management wizard as well. But that's not the case. In fact, all that's required to establish a position of strength as a borrower is, first, a willingness to spend a little time mapping out a personal borrowing strategy, based on the points outlined in this book. Then, when you have your objectives and strategies outlined clearly on paper before you, all it takes to make it all work is the commitment and discipline to act.

For the most part, the true Power Borrower just operates on good, solid common sense. After thinking a little about it, any reasonable, intelligent person will come to most of the same conclusions I've stated in the foregoing pages. Everybody knows, for example, most of these basic principles that underlie much of what we've discussed:

- You shouldn't spend more than you make.
- You should be wary of borrowing from relatives or friends.
- It's best not to cosign a note.
- Don't use loans to pay for your daily living expenses.
- Shop around for the best terms and interest rates.
- Develop a reputation in the business and credit community as a good risk.

These points are certainly nothing more than good old-fashioned common sense. But it's amazing, isn't it, how few people follow these guidelines in practice?

So it's necessary for most of us to examine the basics in some detail and then think through exactly how they apply to us, in each of our individual financial situations. Finally, when we've got the import of these principles straight in our minds, it's incumbent on each of us to put them into practice in our daily lives.

So many of us know what we *should* be doing with our finances. But so few have achieved the status of Power Borrower, where we actually live in a way that demonstrates we're in control of our credit, and ultimately, of the financial side of our lives.